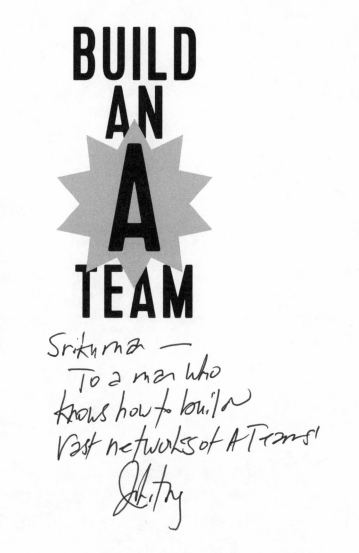

BUILD AN A TEAM

Srikuma —
To a man who
knows how to build
vast networks of A Teams!

Whitny

BUILD
AN
A
TEAM

Play to Their Strengths and
Lead Them Up the Learning Curve

WHITNEY JOHNSON

HARVARD BUSINESS REVIEW PRESS

Boston, Massachusetts

HBR Press Quantity Sales Discounts

Harvard Business Review Press titles are available at significant quantity discounts when purchased in bulk for client gifts, sales promotions, and premiums. Special editions, including books with corporate logos, customized covers, and letters from the company or CEO printed in the front matter, as well as excerpts of existing books, can also be created in large quantities for special needs.

For details and discount information for both print and ebook formats, contact booksales@harvardbusiness.org, tel. 800-988-0886, or www.hbr.org/bulksales.

The web addresses referenced in this book were live and correct at the time of the book's publication but may be subject to change.

Library of Congress Cataloging-in-Publication data is forthcoming.

ISBN: 978-1-63369-364-7
eISBN: 978-1-63369-365-4

The paper used in this publication meets the requirements of the American National Standard for Permanence of Paper for Publications and Documents in Libraries and Archives Z39.48-1992.

To my A-team:
Roger, David, and Miranda

CONTENTS

BUILD AN A TEAM

BEING THE KIND OF BOSS PEOPLE LOVE TO WORK FOR

Happiness lies not in the mere possession of money; it lies in the joy of achievement, in the thrill of creative effort.

—**Franklin D. Roosevelt**

In San Diego, California, in 1953, a new startup set its sights on the Space Age. The Rocket Chemical Company had a small lab and just three people, but they could see a major opportunity in front of them. The aerospace industry was producing incredible new technology—missiles and rockets that could fly farther than any had before—but that technology had a major weakness: it was all made of metal, and metal rusts.

Norm Larsen, the chief chemist, had an idea. He thought he could come up with a chemical compound that would keep the newly invented rockets and missiles from rusting.

The secret would be to find a substance that would simply *displace* the water: stop water from clinging to the metal surfaces of the rockets so it would roll harmlessly away, like water off a duck's back. In his one-room lab, Norm and his two cofounders tried again and again to find a compound that would work. They tried ten times. They tried twenty times. They tried thirty times. Finally, on the fortieth try, Larsen and his team found a successful formula. They were soon producing the product for Convair, a division of General Dynamics and maker of NASA's Atlas missile.

Then something funny happened. The product worked so well that workers at General Dynamics started sneaking it home to use around the house as a protectant, solvent, and all-purpose lubricant. By 1955, Larsen realized he might have a market for his compound that was broader than the aerospace and defense industry. He went back to the lab and started a new set of experiments aimed at finding a way to put his special formula into an aerosol can. In 1959, the first spray cans of the product hit the market, and the world met WD-40.

The product's name comes from "water displacement, fortieth attempt." Not a lot of fanfare or marketing spin behind that one; but forty years later, WD-40 had over 80 percent market share in the multipurpose lubrication market. Today it's practically synonymous with that market, and that yellow and blue can is found in 75 percent of American households. While companies like 3M and Valvoline have tried to unseat WD-40, none has been able to. By one estimate it has staved off competition from more than 200 rival products, including more than a dozen produced by billion-dollar firms.[1]

How does a company stay at the top of its game for over sixty years, making and selling a single product whose formula has only been tweaked once? (In the early 1960s, they tried to improve the smell.) How can a company be successful when its product strategy flies in the face of everything the business establishment normally preaches, like "segment your market" and "diversify"? I'd argue they do it by taking a radical approach to managing their people.

Nationally, only 33 percent of employees are engaged in their work, according to Gallup. Worldwide, those numbers are even worse: just 15 percent of employees say they're engaged.[2] But at WD-40, a whopping 93 percent of employees consider themselves to be engaged in their work, and 97 percent say they are excited about the future of the company.[3] Why the difference?

Because WD-40 practices a human resources strategy that I call "personal disruption." A strategy that is centered around learning: you start as a beginner, embracing the confusion that comes with being a novice; you experience a state of deep engagement as you learn, grow, and gain traction; and you feel the joy of mastery once you get to the top of your learning curve. But then—crucially—you find a new challenge to tackle and the cycle starts over; human beings are wired to learn and change, not to stay in one place, doing the same thing over and over again.

At WD-40, this means that employees have an identifiable career path inside the company and that managers help their employees get from point A to points B, C, and D. WD-40 wants to keep people in house, not chained to their roles.

They encourage employees to learn, leap to new roles, and learn and leap again. Because management encourages leaps to new learning curves, many people have been there for ten to twenty-five years and longer. As CEO Garry Ridge told me, "I get so much joy out of seeing people who are coming through the company and stepping into new roles. They're standing on the edge and I say 'Jump! Don't worry. There's a net . . .'"

No wonder 60 percent of WD-40 employees believe they can satisfy their career objectives without ever leaving the company. Three senior leaders began their careers there in the role of receptionist. "Our brand manager for our key brand started in a part-time position [as receptionist]," says Ridge. "We pushed her and pushed her and she jumped and she jumped, and now she's brand manager of WD-40. That's what we love."

WD-40 exemplifies the practice of developing people through repeated disruptions. Because people are challenged by and engaged in their work, they stay. This impacts the bottom line. WD-40's market capitalization has grown from $250 million to $1.6 billion over the past eighteen years. Not bad for a company that sells a can of oil.[4]

The Power of Personal Disruption

Most of us are not excited about our work. In one survey, 84 percent of employees said they felt "trapped" in their jobs.[5] In another, only 22 percent said they had anything like a clear career path in their current job.[6]

I've heard these complaints firsthand. In 2015 I published *Disrupt Yourself,* a guide to radically reinventing your own career. But as I've traveled in the subsequent months, delivering keynotes, consulting with organizations, and coaching executives on personal disruption, two questions come up more than any others: "How can I get my people to disrupt themselves?" and "How can I get my boss to let me disrupt *my* self?" It's ironic and even sad: both employees and their managers want to experience the growth that can come with disruption, but it's not happening. No wonder true engagement is so rare.

Change, not stasis, is the natural mode of human life. Change promotes growth; stasis results in decline. Whether they are the manager of a small team or the head honcho overseeing thousands of people across several business units, proactive managers get this. They cultivate environments that keep the work experience fresh. They encourage and facilitate personal disruptions. They recognize that the best reward they can give their people—the thing that motivates and engages beyond money or praise—is learning. It's what makes each of us more productive. It's what turns our organizations into talent magnets.

Managers who recognize this not only make a huge difference to their company, but have a direct influence on the lives of their employees. My own experience illustrates this. When I first arrived in Manhattan after college, freshly armed with a not-particularly-useful university degree in music, I needed to work, and I wanted to do something exciting. Wall Street in the late eighties was exciting, but it didn't have openings for pianists, so I started as a secretary at a financial services firm and took business classes at night. After a few years, my boss, Cesar Baez, helped bridge the gap for me to become an investment banker. It was an unusual move, and it laid the groundwork for my entire career.

From there, I went on to become an *Institutional Investor*–ranked equity research analyst for eight consecutive years. I was rated by Starmine as a superior stock picker, following stocks such as América Móvil (NYSE: AMX), Televisa (NYSE: TV), and Telmex (NYSE: TMX), which at the time accounted for roughly 40 percent of the Mexican Stock Exchange's market cap.

But by 2004, I was hankering for a new challenge. I shared with a top executive at my company that I wanted to move into the management track, hoping to enlist his support. Instead, he was dismissive. He had a "We like you right where you are" attitude. In retrospect, I think I could have handled the conversation better. But at the time I remember thinking, "I'm ready for something new, and if it's not going to happen here, I'll have to leave." Within a year, I struck out on my own.

After I left New York, I cofounded an early-stage investment fund with Harvard Business School professor Clayton Christensen called the Disruptive Innovation Fund. It was this work that would lead me to understand that Christensen's theory of disruption could be applied not only to startups but to people's careers as well.

Disruptive innovation, at its simplest, explains how low-end industry insurgents take on—and eventually outcompete—high-end incumbents who seemingly should have known better. Think Toyota in the 1960s. Their product was inferior. Their position was weak. General Motors could have crushed them like a cockroach. But they didn't. Market leaders rarely do. After all, it was just a silly little Corolla. What threat did it pose to the bigger, faster, better, more expensive Cadillac? But once a disruptor gains its footing, it too is motivated by bigger, faster, better. For Toyota that was the Camry, then Lexus. Lexus today has a 16 percent market share in America, twice that of Cadillac.[7]

Christensen and others have found similar examples in health care, steel manufacturing, personal computing, and dozens of other industries. But the pattern is the same: an insurgent firm starts out making a vastly inferior product and sells it to nonconsumers (such as people who can't afford the incumbent's product) or to customers overserved by the expensive bells and whistles attached to the incumbent's offering. Once the insurgent firm gains traction, its growth hockey-sticks upward, letting it also add features, improve quality, and like Pac-Man, eat away at the incumbent firm's market share. By the time a counterattack by the incumbent makes sense, it's too late: the insurgent is too strong, too firmly entrenched to dislodge.

It is now generally accepted that disruptive innovation underpins the invention of new products and services, creates new markets, and amplifies revenue and profits—often in huge ways. Less generally recognized, but equally true, is that personal disruption in the workplace—the movement of people from one learning curve to the next, one challenge to another— can drive learning, engagement, and even innovation.

Managers are the people best placed to shape these learning curves and help employees recognize when it's time to leap to a new curve.

And yet all too often, that kind of clarity of purpose, on-the-job development, and career-shaping mentoring get lost in the day-to-day shuffle of putting out fires, running to meetings, and answering emails. It's not uncommon to hear a manager complain that they have no one who can pick up the slack when they're on vacation but in almost the same breath say they're just too busy to teach employees what to do or dismiss hands-on coaching as hand-holding or babysitting.

This isn't the kind of manager most people set out to be. It's just that the long-term, important task of coaching and developing people gets lost in the chaos of day-to-day to-do lists. And then, when an employee leaves and the manager has an empty role to fill, we are so harried, we hire someone who knows how to do the job today—rather than hire someone who might grow in the role over the course of many tomorrows.

As managers, we have the same dilemma that industry incumbents face: we become great at maximizing efficiency while taking our eye off the ball of personal and professional growth. And that's how we end up with so many people feeling bored or stuck in their jobs, with no clear career path. The result is stagnation, for both the employees and the organization.

An employee, like a startup, requires a certain amount of up-front investment. A good manager, like a good investor, knows how to exercise patience. Having done your due diligence before bringing someone new onboard, you'll have a certain amount of confidence that they'll grow into the role. When they do, you'll be rewarded with the returns: an employee who is highly productive. If you take this approach with your whole "portfolio" of employees, the result will be an A-team: people who are at different stages on their individual learning curves who achieve the "sweet spot" of highly engaged growth at different times.

How This Book Is Organized

In *Build an A-Team*, I lay out a framework for engaging and motivating employees by understanding and managing their individual learning. Chapter 1 explains the basic idea: that a learning curve is shaped like an S. At the low end of the curve is the discomfort (and excitement) of the unknown. At the high end of the curve is the confidence (and dullness) of mastery. In the middle, on the steep part of the curve, is where the magic happens: where employees are happiest, learning quickly and highly engaged.

Chapter 2 gives an overview of seven ways managers can support and accelerate their employees' movement up the learning curve. I'll describe how you can identify where each of your employees is on their personal learning curve and what help they need to climb it—eventually mastering their existing curve and leaping to a new one.

Chapters 3 and 4 explain how to use this approach in hiring and onboarding, respectively: when your employee knows little about their new learning curve. Chapter 5 describes managing the "sweet spot": the steep part of the learning curve, when your employee is maximally engaged and learning fast. Chapter 6 discusses what managers need to know about the period of mastery at the top of the curve. While it sounds great ("Hey, my employee is a master! I'll just stay out of their way!"), this can be a really tricky time. If things become too dull, they'll start looking for a new job. Or worse, become complacent. Chapter 7 describes how to craft new challenges *inside* your company. Finally, chapter 8 discusses some of the mental challenges and other roadblocks that can get in your way as you apply this approach.

Managing people so they can disrupt themselves honors the biology of change that is our human nature. We each have a life cycle, made up of myriad smaller life cycles. Beginnings and endings, growth and decline; we cannot stay the same.

Our work life—so large a part of the whole—is like this too. Individual jobs have a life span. They have a first day of work and, if we are wise, a last day. This opens the door for our talented employees to continue to grow with us and for us, rather than constantly turning these valuable assets over to other employers.

Because we are always evolving, one of the great frustrations we can encounter is the perception that nothing is changing around us. That our organic human life is rolling along in a static landscape like a car in an old movie jostling against a painted background. How can we help but become disengaged and detached when we feel like actors on a set that never alters, where Act I is never succeeded by Act II or III? It is not enough to do our work with the latest gadgets and hot-off-the-press technology. Bright shiny objects lose their sheen quickly. The work itself needs to change: problems to solve, needs to address, brain-stimulating challenges must roll around again—and on a regular basis.

We can only rummage through the same rocks for so long and still find diamonds. Eventually it's time to swing our pick into the solid wall of the unknown and begin the work of discovery anew.

THE S CURVE OF LEARNING

To boldly go where no man has gone before.

—*Star Trek*'s Captain James Kirk

Captain James Cook was one of the greatest explorers and cartographers in history. He was the first European to visit what is now Sydney, Australia. He discovered the Hawaiian Islands and skirted Antarctica, sailing a total of well over two hundred thousand miles—essentially the distance from the earth to the moon. One-third of the globe was unmapped when he was born; when he died in 1779, he had explored most of it and drawn maps so accurate that they were still in use two hundred years later.[1]

It's unlikely Cook would have accomplished any of this had he not been willing to jump to new learning curves and been sponsored by people who recognized and invested in his talent.

Cook was born in 1728 to an impoverished laboring family in Yorkshire, England, and raised in a tiny hovel where only one of his five siblings lived to adulthood. The lord of the local manor, Thomas Scottowe, recognized James as gifted and paid for him to be educated at the local school. At seventeen, Cook moved to the coast of the North Sea, and thanks to his patron's recommendation, he secured a job as an assistant shopkeeper.

When the sea called to him, Cook found a mentor in James Walker, a ship owner and coal merchant, who took Cook on as his apprentice. Under Walker's tutelage, he worked his way up the ranks of the merchant navy, while studying mathematics, navigation, and astronomy.

In 1755, Walker offered Cook the position of ship's master. Instead, he chose to join the Royal Navy where he began as a common sailor. (With a war in France looming, he believed this step back would lead to opportunities for promotion.) Here he found another patron in Hugh Palliser, an aspiring officer who was impressed with Cook's talents and brought him along as he ascended within the naval establishment.

Cook's mapmaking skills and his leadership during the Seven Years' War eventually earned him the command of the HMS *Endeavor*, the Royal Navy research vessel he would captain on his legendary voyages.

Cook's success depended on three men—Scottowe, Walker, and Palliser—who recognized his gifts and helped develop them. Without these talent-spotting sponsors, instead of becoming a revered adventurer, he might have wasted away in obscure poverty.

Captain James Cook wrote in his journal that he had "sailed farther than any other man before me." Captain

James T. Kirk, the pop culture icon of *Star Trek*, is modeled on Cook, and his motto "to boldly go where no man has gone before" could easily have belonged to Cook.

This is what people want on the job: to boldly go where they haven't gone before. To venture into uncharted territory. To take themselves and their company where they've never been.

And yet, we humans also like a certain amount of predictability. If given the chance to see our future in a crystal ball, most of us would peek. We like to flip a switch and the light goes on. When we can forecast the future, we elevate our sense of security. When we believe we control our circumstances, we feel more confident. Even millennials, who often hummingbird from one opportunity to the next, believe that sticking with one company and climbing the corporate ladder is a safer bet for salary growth than switching jobs or entrepreneurship.[2] But, control is an illusion. None of us knows what the future will bring.

It's a conundrum. Disruption fosters innovation. It also challenges current, and often dearly held, practices without providing clear alternatives. It's especially murky when it comes to finding the best way to manage your employees.

This is where the S curve model comes in. At the Disruptive Innovation Fund we employed an S curve model, popularized by sociologist E. M. Rogers, in our investment decision making. In investing, the S curve model is used to gauge how quickly an innovation will be adopted and how rapidly it will penetrate a market. The S curve helps make the unpredictable predictable. At the base of the S, progress

FIGURE 1-1

The S curve of learning

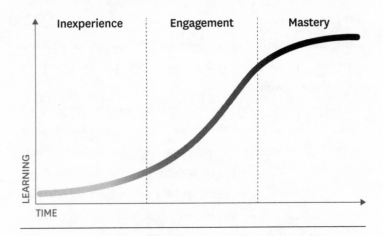

is relatively slow until a tipping point is reached—the knee of the curve. This is followed by hypergrowth up the steep back of the curve until slow growth occurs again, as market saturation leads to a flattening top of the S. (See figure 1-1, "The S curve of learning," for a visual representation.)

The S curve model also helps us understand the development of and shifts in individual careers. S curve math tells us that the early days of a role, at the low end of the S, can feel like a slog. Cause and effect are seemingly disconnected. Huge effort yields little. Understanding this helps avoid discouragement.

As we put in days, weeks, and months of practice, we will speed up and move up the S curve, roaring into competence and the confidence that accompanies it. This is the exhilarating part of the S curve, where all our neurons are firing. It's the sweet spot.

As we approach mastery, tasks become easier and easier. This is satisfying for a while, but because we are no longer enjoying the feel-good effects of learning, we are likely to get bored. If we stay on the top of a curve too long, our plateau becomes a precipice.

Everyone Has an S Curve

In one of my facilitated sessions, a CEO said to me, "Eighty percent of my people don't have an S curve. They just don't care." I could hear the frustration in his voice; it was real. But his claim wasn't true. There are different types of curves and factors that can affect them, but everyone has an S curve. And throughout a career, most of us will discover several or even many of them.

If employees "don't care," it doesn't mean that they don't have an S curve—it means they are disengaged. Nearly every human being is on the lookout for growth opportunities. If a person can't grow with a company, they will grow away from it. As with any rule, there are exceptions. Some are people who won't grow, no matter how you try to help them. But what about past high performers who are currently underperforming? If it's time to jump, and they won't, you may need to give them a nudge.

Think of the leaven in bread: a little bit is all it takes for the whole mass of dough to rise, but let it rise too long and it will collapse. The energy of the chemical reaction will have spent itself. The key is to capture the leavening at the right time, bake our loaves, and reserve some "starter" for the next batch. The energy of your employees is there waiting to be tapped. But they will need to start over regularly. Ensure that they can, and they will provide lift to your organization—and do it over and over again.

Saul Kaplan, founder of the Business Innovation Factory, once told me, "My life has been about searching for the steep learning curve because that's where I do my best work: swinging like Tarzan from one curve to the next." This is true for most of us. If we want our employees to keep working at a high level, the S curve management strategy is key.

An A-Team Is a Collection of Learning Curves

Just as an investor's portfolio has diversified holdings (e.g., you don't put all your money into a single company), your team should include employees who are at different phases of development. Visualize your team as a collection of people at different points on their own personal S curves. Aim for an optimal mix of low-, middle-, and high-end-of-the-curve employees: roughly 15 percent at the low end, around 70 percent of the team in the sweet spot middle, and 15 percent at the high end of the curve.

Assume that new team members will be at the low end of their curve for approximately six months—although this will vary, of course, depending on the difficulty of the role and the aptitude of the individual. At the six-month mark, they should be hitting the tipping point and moving onto the sleek, steep back of their learning curve. During this second phase, they'll reach peak productivity, which is where they should stay for three to four years. At around the four-year mark, they will have made the push into mastery. In the mastery phase, an employee performs every task with ease and confidence. This top-of-the-curve, high-ender can mentor new team members who are surfing the low end of the wave. But ease, and even confidence, can quickly deteriorate into boredom without the motivation of a new challenge. Before long, it will be time for them to jump to a new learning curve.

Mapping Your Team's S Curve

We've developed a diagnostic tool to help you determine where you, your team members, and even your potential hires might fall on an S curve. The S-Curve Locator (SCL) is available on my website at (whitneyjohnson.com/diagnostic). It's helpful for each team member to see if the results square with what they expected. If they don't, it's useful to ask why. The aggregate results, from a managerial standpoint, provide a snapshot of latent talent and capacity for innovation.

Consider a global health care company. After administering the SCL to nearly one thousand employees, we found that around 5 percent were at the low end of the curve. This phase is characterized by a high degree of challenge, intense stretching, and personal growth. Seventy-one percent of respondents fell into the central portion of the S curve, indicating that they were challenged, with room for continued learning and growth. One-quarter (24 percent) of respondents were at the high end of the curve, suggesting a level of mastery that may demand a new opportunity to help them stay engaged. While a manager could be forgiven for thinking that's a good thing, 24 percent is too high in my experience. These valuable employees have moved beyond the sweet spot into a potential danger zone. Most of them didn't want to leave the firm for something new. Most expressed excitement about the company's mission and values. But 40 percent of the employees were feeling under-challenged. For a manager, this is an important data point. If you have too many people at the high end, it's a surefire sign that you are at risk of disruption. People at the high end of the curve may be high performers, but if they stay there too long, they will get bored, and leave, or become complacent. Companies with bored and complacent people don't innovate; they get disrupted. On the flip side, a large percentage of people at the high end of the curve presents an opportunity: to capitalize on innovative capacity lying dormant.

By contrast, at WD-40, the company with the amazing engagement scores profiled in the introduction, my assessment produced the balance of numbers we would anticipate from an engaged workplace: a small number (5.6 percent) of employees scored in the lower range of the diagnostic, indicating that they may be dealing with the high-challenge portion of the S curve and the struggle to gain competence. The majority (88.3 percent) fell within the sweet spot of high engagement and productivity, indicating that they are learning, feeling challenged, and enjoying growth in their present role. A relatively small number (6.1 percent) of employees are operating at the higher end of the S curve, indicating a level of mastery that may require a new, more challenging path. An additional 5 percent of people were closing in on this mastery stage.

To be clear, not all employees on the high end of the S curve will need to jump. While some high-end employees may have fallen into a rut of complacency and entitlement, some may be able to stay in their current role longer if given stretch assignments. Especially in intellectually rigorous fields, where it may require years for true mastery. So long as we are aware that tedium can undercut performance, we can watch for signs that an employee needs to jump. We'll talk more about the high end of the curve in chapters 6 and 7.

Chess, Not Checkers

Chess is the quintessential strategic game. Instead of having one type of playing piece on the board that represents you, there are many—there's a whole team. Unlike in checkers, in which many pieces on the board all do the same thing, chess pieces are defined by specific roles. They are designed to move differently and yet work together. A good chess player both understands the individual moves of different pieces and knows how to deploy them in complementary ways.

As leaders, we see the whole board and understand the roles of different individuals. The team objective is achieved when we optimally coordinate these people's roles, always visualizing several moves ahead.

Of course, there are a few flaws with this analogy. The people we employ are not inanimate objects but rather free agents—free to leave our board and go play for someone else. Nor do they have a limited set of prescribed moves. The roles they fill may initially provide an opportunity for them to contribute but may ultimately become limiting. Within an S curve is potential, but eventually that potential is exhausted. As managers, we want to recognize when someone who has been functioning in one role is ready to try something new. Consider the pawn that makes its way across the board and is rewarded by becoming a queen. It's a powerful augmentation of the pawn's abilities—and of the chess player's options.

Jim Skinner, former CEO of McDonald's, is a good example of such a "pawn." Skinner completely lacked the standard CEO credentials. He didn't have an MBA—he never even graduated from college. His first job was flipping burgers. But over four decades, he was able to assume a variety of roles that eventually led to the C-suite. When his predecessor stepped down due to health problems, he got the top job. McDonald's did well during his tenure, but Skinner's most enduring contribution may be his emphasis on talent development. Perhaps because he didn't have college credentials himself, the training and development of his employees was something Skinner took very seriously. He created a leadership institute a year after he became CEO and required that all executives train at least two potential successors—one who could do the job today, the "ready now," in McDonald's parlance, and one who could be a future replacement, the "ready future."[3]

Limiting people to certain roles or positions holds no benefits for your business. Be the chess master that provides vision and coordination while allowing pieces to move them-selves. Alan Mulally, former CEO of Ford, began his career at Boeing. A strong performer, he had been promoted from individual contributor to manager. After a few months, one of Mulally's direct reports, a talented engineer, announced he was quitting. When Mulally asked why, the engineer said, "You micromanage. You've made fourteen changes to my work. Your job is not to do my job. Your job is to help me understand the bigger picture. Plug me into the network. Advocate for me." The employee still quit. Mulally, who went on to be one the best CEOs of our time, apparently learned his lesson.[4]

Eager, capable employees tackling new challenges are a key driver of innovation within an organization. Author Alex Haley once said, "When an old person dies it's like a library burning."[5] When employees leave a firm, books burn: we lose a wealth of vital institutional knowledge and expertise. Let's not be the innovation book burners in our organizations.

What You Measure Matters

We tend to want or even expect the development work to already be done when someone enters our employment. Why then would we reward people who focus on develop-ing talent? We wouldn't. With expertise as a given, we focus on numbers and are rewarded for doing so. Just look at the metrics. Number of widgets sold: check. Number of clients or customers called: check. Number of people developed? None. Number of people poached? None. These metrics aren't considered. Instinctively you know they should be, but you still ignore them. It's no wonder we're reluctant to reward managers for the development of resources that happen to be human.

If we are to embrace the power of personal disruption through carefully orchestrated jumps to new S curves, we'll rethink the way we evaluate those who manage the take-offs and landings. A simple start is to create metrics that reward talent spotters and developers. Jo Taylor, director of Let's Talk Talent, a talent-management consultancy, shared several ideas that she applied during her three-year stint as director of talent management at Talk Talk, a UK-based telecom. "Include talent development in senior managers' performance review matrix, and tell them that a percentage of their bonus is going to be payable only if they've developed their people. You can measure that through 360 reviews from direct reports. Using those reviews, you can also quickly assess which individual managers are doing this kind of development, and focus on those who aren't with additional training and resources."

Talk Talk also set a high target for internal mobility within the company: they wanted to see 60 percent of available roles filled internally. The company's philosophy was that the business—not individual managers—owns the talent, which encouraged and incentivized managers to develop talented people and allow them to move into new roles internally. The stats from the beginning of Taylor's tenure at Talk Talk compared with the numbers when she left her position suggest that talent development and internal mobility increase employee engagement: internal mobility increased from 35 percent to 50 percent; employee engagement increased from 56 percent to 76 percent; the company's profitability was up from $1.30 to $3.00 a share.

Another way to figure out who is developing talent is to first analyze who is delivering results, getting promoted, and going on to interesting opportunities, and then ask those people who they work for. If past employees have been more likely to quit than jump to new curves, that's a danger sign. Management thinker Dave Ulrich said it well: "Instead of asking a multi-millionaire how many millions they've earned, ask how many millionaires they have created." For example, Lori Leibovich, editor in chief of the Health brand at Time Inc., has managed and developed several journalists who have gone on to land prestigious jobs in the field, including a writer at large for *New York* magazine and executive editor at *Cosmopolitan*, to name a few. This is someone people want to work for. Who in your organization has a track record of apprenticing talent?

When I was an equity research analyst at Merrill Lynch, some great people worked for me. Like Mike Kopelman. When an opportunity arose to work for Jessica Reif Cohen, the leading media analyst globally—she covered companies like News Corp—I suggested and brokered a move for Mike. It was a huge loss to me and my team, but a boon to Merrill Lynch overall. Unlike at Talk Talk, though, talent development wasn't a metric measured in performance reviews. At Merrill Lynch, managers were developing talent at their own risk. If you want managers to let their people grow, reward them for it.

Hire Self-Starters

Kim Sreng Richardson arrived in the United States from a refugee camp in Cambodia at age twelve, unable to speak, read, or write English. She was placed with nine-year-olds at first but soon caught up and graduated from high school at age nineteen. At twenty-three, she started work at CPS Technologies, a materials manufacturer in Norton, Massachusetts, as an entry-level assembly operator in the factory. After six months, she saw an opportunity to move into quality assurance. She didn't know anything about Word, Excel, or Access, all of which she needed to complete the inspection documentation. But she was willing to figure them out, and CPS provided training so she was able learn. She says, "When I go to work, I give a hundred percent all the time. I'm hungry. And then I get the opportunity." This has happened repeatedly for two decades. Today, she runs CPS's manufacturing operations. CEO Grant Bennett says of her, "Sometimes Kim raises her hand. Sometimes she is tapped. Either way, we always know she will get the job done. She is one of the most capable people I know."

Richardson's story highlights an important prerequisite for this personal disruption approach to managing: it only works if you're managing people who can self-manage. You need people who believe that what they do makes a difference and are willing to hold themselves accountable, independent of constant oversight. *Do they arrive on time? Are they prepared for meetings?* These are clues as to their level of personal responsibility. An effective manager will want to give such self-starting, self-monitoring, self-governing high performers the opportunity to move to new S curves.

During a restructuring at Novartis, Henna Inam shared with her boss that she had her eye on a general manager (GM) slot. (Restructurings are frequently seedbeds for personal disruption.) As a warm-up, they wanted her to do a rotation in sales, selling Gerber products to Walmart. Her manager for this rotation was Gary Pinkowski. For a numbers-oriented Wharton grad like Inam, Pinkowski's leadership style was unexpected. During their one-on-one conversations, he asked only three questions: How are you? How are your people? And, How is the business? Pinkowski's high-level vision and approach were evident in the number (only three) and the tenor (people first and second) of his questions.

Within three years, Inam was up for GM, with a choice of assignments: the opportunity to take over a sales leadership position for Novartis selling into Walmart—a billion-dollar business—or become the GM for Mexico, a $100 million business. The assignment in Mexico wasn't as high profile, but it would give her the opportunity to run an entire business, including the commercial and R&D (research and development) functions. It would also leverage one of her strengths— cultural adaptability, developed through living in five countries across three continents. She chose the opportunity in Mexico, and in taking on this challenge, Inam now reported to Tim Strong, known for his trusting, hands-off management. Two years later, she had turned around the business in Mexico and was one of ten people out of ninety thousand employees who received an award for her outstanding performance.

Antony Jay, a former BBC executive, posits that retaining high-performing talent relies on the decentralization of leadership. It's important to encourage employees to be founders in their own space, to give them the chance to make what they will. "The conventional management hierarchy," writes Jay, "is rather like an enclosed city state: a young manager looks around and sees the mountains that circumscribe ambition." Circumscribed ambition is a hotbed of disengagement: talented people will either leave or be forced, unhappily, to accept the unsatisfactory conditions that limit them. "Corporation executives may tell you that an organization cannot have too many good managers, but they are wrong. What it cannot do is keep them good without constantly giving them tasks that match up to their abilities." Assign and reassign "to make sure that staff of high quality stays with the firm—and stays of high quality."

Managing a team as a collection of individual S curves implies a decentralization of power. People should be able to function independently enough that, with minimal oversight, they can both operate for the good of the whole and make their own fortune. "The real pleasure of power is the pleasure of freedom," says Jay.[6]

Think about your best boss. Like Henna Inam's former bosses, Tim Strong, and Gary Pinkowski, now VP of sales at Post Foods, your best boss made it possible for you to succeed, confident that once you knew the rules, you could self-manage. When you facilitate personal disruption, you build an A-team and become a boss people want to work for. A boss people love.

Summary

The S curve, traditionally used to model the dispersion of innovative goods and services in the marketplace, is also a helpful model for understanding and planning career disruptions.

The S curve represents three distinct phases of disruption:

1. The low end, involving a challenging and sometimes slow push for competence.

2. The up-swinging back of the curve, where competence is achieved and progress is rapid.

3. The high end of the curve, where competence has evolved into mastery and can quickly devolve into boredom and disengagement.

This necessitates disruption to a new curve to reengage and maintain employee productivity. Poor engagement levels are consistently a challenge to business growth and profitability.

Create a team that is a high-functioning collection of S curves, with a small percentage of people at the low and high ends of the curve and the majority in the sweet spot at any given time.

THE SEVEN ACCELERANTS OF LEARNING AND GROWTH

> Disruptive movement must come from within.
>
> —Leo Tolstoy

Consider a chunk of broken asphalt—a road full of potholes. At some point, there was a hairline fracture, tiny, certainly not worthy of repair. There was rain or melting snow. Water seeped into the asphalt, froze, and expanded—and the asphalt broke.

Asphalt has enormous compression strength: it can withstand thousands of pounds of surface or external pressure. So why did it break? Because it has far less *tensile* strength. It can't withstand pressure from within.

People are a bit like asphalt. We can handle a lot of external pressure. If this gives us the strength to persevere, that can be a good thing. If we resist and batten down the hatches when faced with the inevitable, it's not.

What happens if the pressure comes from within? What if you have the courage, or even the pressing need to try something new? To ride, rather than resist, the wave of disruption? This is where the relative weakness of tensile strength can work in your favor. Just a few small changes, like drops of water, permeate, expand, and break your hold on the past, creating space for a new and better version of you.

In my book *Disrupt Yourself*, I outlined the seven-stage process of personal disruption. Because we'll refer to these seven points throughout this book, I'll include them here so they are all in one place. I'll also explain how they apply to you as a manager. While it is true that change must come from within, there's a lot you can do from the outside to help your employees along.

Identify the Right Risks

The low end of an S curve is an uncomfortable, risky place. Everything is new, there is so much to learn, and progress can be slow, sometimes for quite a while (we'll talk more about this in chapter 4). Your new hire is stretching, working at the edge of their abilities. As a manager, it's easy to become impatient or nervous about their rate of progress. You may even doubt the hiring decision.

You can mitigate this doubt by taking the right kinds of risk.

There are two kinds of risk to consider: competitive risk and market risk.

Competitive risk involves head-to-head competition. How successfully can you compete against ten, twenty, even fifty applicants for a single big opportunity? Or against six similarly qualified peers vying for a promotion? This is brutal math; the ratio of winners to losers is daunting.

Market risk, however, is about creating entirely new arenas of competition. There may be no official job posting or even an established position. But you detect a gap and articulate a way to fill it: with a new job, tailor-made for your expertise. You may be told "no thanks," but if a manager says "yes please" to your idea, there is no competition for the spot. There is a risk of being denied but not of being outmatched.

Sarah Feingold, general counsel at car seller Vroom, shared with me how she landed her previous role as senior counsel at online retailer Etsy. In addition to being an attorney, Feingold is an accomplished custom jewelry-maker. She had been selling her pieces on Etsy, learned they were changing their legal policies, and decided to write to the customer service team and offer advice pro bono. When they brushed her off, she recounts, "I said, 'You know what? Why don't I just speak with your founder?' They gave me his number. We spoke for about a half an hour. When I hung up the phone, I thought, 'This company is amazing. I love this company. I can add value. And they clearly can use the value I can add.'

I booked a JetBlue ticket and called the founder back. 'I'm coming down for an interview, I said. 'You need in-house legal counsel, and you need it to be me.'"[1]

People gravitate toward competitive risk because it seems safer. It's known. We *know* there is a job available: that's got to be less risky than a job that doesn't yet exist. It seems counterintuitive, but according to disruption theory, this risk assessment is flawed.[2]

Managers are not immune to the lure of certainty. Vacant positions are frequently advertised the same way they were the last time we hired, without the slightest evaluation of what the job calls for. The result being that new employees are often brought in to do a job that a current employee has, out of necessity, already started doing. There is now an overlap, a duplication of effort, that causes your people to butt heads. When you put people in competition with one another who are supposed to be on the same team, failure, at some level, is almost guaranteed.

Each employee (and each manager) requires an individual curve to climb. In hiring for, or moving an employee to, a new role, skew toward market risk whenever possible. What needs aren't being met on your team or in your business? Does it make sense to redistribute responsibilities among current team members? Create a new role? Would more high-quality candidates be available if you looked beyond the margins of a currently available job?

If you assume market risk and deploy employees where no one else is playing, you will improve the odds of your workers' (and your own) success.

Play to Individuals' Distinctive Strengths

When I asked a group of 100 people in a large multinational how many of them played to their strengths on the job, less than 5 percent raised their hands. This was unusually low as straw polls go, but still indicative.

To perform at the highest level, each member of your team must operate from a position of personal strength. I'm not talking about the strengths of the team in general but of each individual's *distinctive* strengths. What does each person do well that other people on the team do not, and what sorts of problems do those strengths equip them to solve? As a manager, your job is to pinpoint what people do uniquely well and pit these abilities against assignments that make their strengths relevant. This powerful combination (abilities + assignments) busts through the challenging low end of the learning curve.

Don't assume people know what their strengths are. Usually, we have a tough time spotting our own superpowers. Because these are things you do reflexively well, like breathing, your strengths are often invisible. And you dismiss them: it's human nature to undervalue what comes easily. Which is why sometimes we hire people into the wrong roles. Because they include on their résumé what they worked hard to do, not what they do without thinking. Identify your reports' strengths—their superpowers, their genius—and play to them.

Be aware too that if your reports aren't strong in the ways you are, you may be blind to their strengths. Walter O'Brien, founder of Scorpion Computer Services and the inspiration for the television show *Scorpion*, was a child prodigy who started programming computers at age nine. He went on to compete in the World Olympics of Informatics and placed sixth in the world at age 18. O'Brien started his company to help people solve problems (originally they were mostly technical problems, but the company's mission has expanded over the years to take on a wide range of other challenges).

From the beginning, O'Brien hired people who were like him: technology geniuses with high IQs. "I thought having a company full of geniuses was a good idea," he says. "I was wrong. When I put two geniuses on the same project, they tried to kill each other, all while insulting the customer. That's when I started to realize there was a thing called EQ—emotional intelligence—[that involved] common sense and social skills. Often the higher the IQ, the lower the EQ. So I needed to go get some of that EQ stuff."[3] Recognizing he needed people who were strong in ways he wasn't, O'Brien started hiring single moms, elementary school teachers, psychologists—people with skills such as self-awareness, empathy, and the ability to manage conflict. These high-EQ employees liaise between Scorpion's high-IQ technology specialists and its clients and are nicknamed "Super Nannies." It's important to play to your strengths, like being a computer genius. But in a room full of computer geniuses, the distinctive strength is emotional intelligence. Play to your people's distinctive strengths, encourage them to play where others aren't, and you'll create a flywheel for climbing the S curve of learning.

Impose Thoughtful Constraints

Constraint is a word that tends to evoke a negative response. We want unlimited, unbounded freedom. Or so we think.

Consider gravity, a constant, unseen, but potent constraint. If we want to manipulate the strictures of gravity, it's a given we'll need to innovate. We invent parachutes, hang gliders, and hot air balloons. We master aerodynamics and the chemistry of jet fuel. Experiment with rocket propulsion and more.

Constraints work the same way within our organizations. At the low end of a new curve, constraint is almost inevitable. There may be inadequate expertise, buy-in, or funding. These limitations can halt progress. Or they can force us to be resourceful. This act of creation propels us up the learning curve.

Kelly Hoey was working in professional development at the global law firm White & Case. After four years, she'd outgrown her role. She and her boss, Timm Whitney, discussed her options, roles that were open and ones she might create. They weighed numerous factors, from career paths to budgets to politics. She settled on the job of rebuilding a global alumni program which had previously launched with fanfare, but failed due to lack of follow-up. It was an enormous task, allocated virtually zero resources—except Kelly. No budget. No staff. No reliable database. Faced with this meaty new challenge, Kelly's creativity came to the fore. She found ways to track and collect data on alums. Though it was the early days of social media, she figured out how to leverage it. Eighteen months later, Kelly had connected a disengaged audience.

For a management team that already feels long on challenges and short on resources, the idea that people cycle through a new role every three to four years may feel onerous. Why would you want a person to move on when they are at their best? Because "best" is temporary. After three to four years, most employees won't continue to perform at their highest level without a change in the scope of their activities. Timm Whitney, Kelly Hoey's boss, understood this. Even the sharpest knife grows dull through repetitious use.

Time Constraints

I crave—and that is not too strong a word—a free workday to focus on whatever I want. No calls. No pending deadlines. No emails that need to be answered. But when that coveted free day arrives, I get anxious. *What will I do? I have so much to do. I'm late. For what? I don't even know.* I can fritter away hours. On good days, I manage the anxiety by breaking my day up into smaller time units. I'll schedule an hour, even a half hour, of writing, for example. Then I'll take a break: walk around the block. When I give myself a time constraint, such as one hour to work on a project, my productivity soars.

The same is true when we are managing people. When we try to keep a good thing going well beyond its pull date, the law of diminishing returns is in play. Think of what we know about food. Our first bite of a food is the most enjoyable, according to Pierre Chandon, a professor of marketing at INSEAD, but our *last* bite is the one that determines how we felt about the overall experience of eating it. If we eat too much, that last bite isn't very satisfying, and what might have been a positive dining experience becomes far less enjoyable.[4]

These attributes have their equivalent in the workplace. People often share with me that they made a job change because their gut told them it was time. They remembered the pleasure of trying something new and wanted to have that feeling again. Others ignored their gut, wooed by job security, compensation, or benefits. Work became increasingly unpleasant, even painful. The overall experience, though it began well, was remembered negatively.

In any given role, there is a "best by" date for an employee. To maximize that person's value, break their tenure into time segments: the first three months, the second three months. What needs to be accomplished for them to tip into the sweet spot of the curve after roughly six months? Once they are moving into confident competence, what do you want them to accomplish in those three peak performance years? Knowing that things don't get better forever, establish clear expectations around the achievement of mastery. For example, what knowledge do they need to transfer before graduating to the next in-house opportunity? The bonus is that training is shouldered by several people, not just you, their manager.

There are exceptions to the general rule of three years. Franz Busse, formerly of MIT's Lincoln Laboratory and now the CTO of the startup Hala Systems, is a rocket scientist. He believes that his domain, and a few others, such as neurosurgery, are so intellectually rigorous and rapidly evolving that "in three years, [practitioners] still don't know nearly enough to make the right decisions." In these cases, the S curve has a long, shallow, slow back, rather than a steep one. It may take an entire career to exhaust it. The refreshment provided by disruption can be achieved through new projects, assignments, and team configurations. The key is variety. As with a farmer rotating crops or a dog breeder introducing a new bloodline.

Exceptions aside, the mandate is clear: three to six months to get up to speed, three to four years to contribute, three to six months to help others get up to speed. Focus and productivity are the fruit of short stints. By adding the constraint of time to the S curve of each role we manage, we can expect better individual performance and higher-functioning teams.

Expertise Constraints

When we consciously create teams with people at the low, middle, and high end of the S curve, we accept that at any given time, up to 15 percent of our team will be at the low end—a built-in constraint of inexperience. These employees may be struggling or unsure. We will need to practice patience as people move, sometimes slowly, up the curve. This lack of competence can be offset by the novel perspective new hires bring to the table. Their ideas may seem naive or even arrogant at times—they haven't yet earned the right to question. But their vantage point of being new, and the ability to question that comes with it, will be brief. Entertain their suggestions. It can bring enormous value to your team.

Liz Wiseman is a former Oracle executive and *New York Times* best-selling author of the book *Multipliers: How the Best Leaders Make Everyone Smarter.* When Wiseman was just a year out of business school, she was tasked with building a corporate university for Oracle, then a scrappy young software company. "Because I lacked experience, I stayed close to my stakeholders, eagerly seeking guidance from product experts and senior leaders," she says. "The obvious gap between the size of the job and the length of my experience forced me to leverage all available resources. What my team and I lacked in experience and conviction we compensated for with our willingness to learn, to think creatively, and to deliver quick wins to prove ourselves." Within a year, Wiseman was asked to expand Oracle University to serve more than one hundred countries around the world.[5] Inexperience was her tool of creation.

The other side of the expertise coin is that because people know they are going to be in their role for a limited amount of time, once they reach the top of the S curve, there will be an urgency to share what they know so the tribal memory remains intact.

Constraints can feel adversarial, a challenger to all the good things we might accomplish. But when properly embraced, they provide structure that liberates us from chaos, reducing the waste of time and money that results when resources are too liberal. When we welcome constraint as friend, not foe, we keep our energy in reserve for the battle against entitlement, the *true* enemy of growth.

Fight Entitlement at Every Turn

Entitlement is the sneaky saboteur of an S curve climb. It comes in many guises. Like when things aren't fair. And at some point, they aren't. On the merits, we deserved a promotion, a raise, or credit for our good idea, and didn't get it. So we decide the universe is in our debt. Self-absorbed, we backslide.

Then there's the flip side of this: This privileged position should always be our lot. As we give the right people, on the right part of their curve, hard problems to solve, our team will hum with innovative energy. It's human nature to start believing this is the way things will and should always be. *I've built this team. I deserve a fiefdom.* Now worried that the loss of a star performer will dim our prospects, we become talent hoarders.

Our best self will let people grow, even help them go. Raju Narisetti, CEO of Gizmodo Media, who has previously worked in senior leadership for News Corp, the *Wall Street Journal*, and the *Washington Post*, says, "I've increasingly measured myself by saying, 'Where are the people that I've hired? What have they gone on to do . . . ?' I'm proud of the people who are doing bigger, greater things now."[6] Stockpiling people and rationing talent may boost your team for a time, but it cheats your business overall. Aspire to be the boss who sees people not only for who they are, but who they can become. Become known as a talent developer, and when that talent moves on, there will be even more great talent around the corner.

As you lead your team up their learning curve, contending with your own sense of entitlement—also watch out for theirs. More skills will equal more confidence. But they still aren't masters. The word "sophomore" comes from the conjunction of two Greek words, wisdom and foolishness; a sophomore is literally a "wise fool." And that's where your employees are as they start to climb out of the low-end learning curve: They know a little, but they don't know enough.

Fearing an increased sense of entitlement, managers sometimes dial back on praise. Instead, turn the volume up. Consultants Jack Zenger and Joe Folkman reviewed some ten thousand 360-degree assessments and found that the best managers give a mix of praise and criticism. Sounds obvious—except that the people who saw themselves as great managers (but were not seen that way by their employees) tended to give mostly criticism.[7]

Our employees are desperate for praise. And we rarely give it, in part because genuine praise is hard to give.[8] Gretchen Rubin helps explain why. She wrote *The Happiness Project*, a book based on her yearlong initiative to be happier, inspired by Benjamin Franklin's self-improvement efforts. As she set out on this journey, Rubin set the goal to "give positive reviews." "People who are critical are often perceived to be more discerning," Rubin writes. Various studies conclude ". . . that people tend to think that someone who criticizes them is smarter than they are. Although enthusiasm seems easy and undiscriminating, in fact, it's much harder to embrace something than to disdain it. It's riskier." Rubin suggests, "Enthusiasm is a form of social courage . . . Giving positive reviews requires humility . . . A willingness to be pleased requires modesty and even innocence . . . "[9]

Smart managers will learn to be enthusiastic and encourage their team members without entitling them. It's a delicate balance. Focus on praising what is within a team member's control, such as effort expended and a willingness to play nicely with others. Be stingier in extolling the attributes that are not under the individual's control: native talents, appearance, the various manifestations of good fortune. These are the things that most often lead to an outsize sense of privilege.

Disruptive innovation thrives in an environment of gratitude, rather than one of entitlement. This may explain the high percentage of successful immigrant entrepreneurs. In 2010, more than 40 percent of the *Fortune* 500 companies included an immigrant or the child of an immigrant among its founders. It may be that coming from other places and cultures makes them less jaded or blinded by personal privilege and more appreciative of a wide-open playing field in which to make their mark. Life is not accommodating. Work is not accommodating—luckily for us. A constant flow of gratification isn't conducive to moving up the S curve. It distracts us from disturbing the universe.

Stepping Backward Is a Way to Move Forward

When Michelle McKenna-Doyle became CIO (Chief Information Officer) of the NFL (National Football League), she observed that a lot of her people were struggling, not because they weren't talented but because they weren't "slotted to their strengths." She did a deep analysis and started switching seats. But this meant that some people felt they were taking a step back. John Cave, VP of football technology, for example, could create products and build things. However, he didn't have time to do this because he was responsible for all systems development, including enterprise systems. "Why was he weighed down with the payroll system when he could figure out how to evolve the game through technology?" McKenna-Doyle asked. She envisioned a better fit for him.

The NFL wanted to make it easier for coaches to talk to each other during a game. McKenna-Doyle tasked Cave with making this happen. "At first, he was concerned because his overall span was shrinking. 'Just trust me,' I said, 'You're going to be a great innovator.' And he is." John Cave is now even more integral to the football operation, providing top value to the NFL. It's not organizational disruption but personal disruption that drives innovation. Managers who can pair skill sets with problems to be solved are invaluable in initiating this disruption.[10]

In researching this book, I posted the question on LinkedIn: "Who was your best boss?" Among the many respondents (It seems there are a lot of great bosses in the world!)

was Vikas Bagri, social media and civic innovation adviser for the government of Chhattisgarh, India. Within a few weeks, I was sitting in the Chicago office of Vikas's former boss: Sam Pitroda. Pitroda, as it happens, is one of the world's great business leaders and entrepreneurial thinkers. He was instrumental in telecom and technology development in India, a onetime adviser to former Indian prime minister Rajiv Gandhi, and the holder of over a hundred international patents. During Pitroda's stint at the helm of C-DOT (Center for the Development of Telematics) in India, over the course of a few months, several employees announced they were going to pursue additional study in the United States. Their managers were so angry they wanted to fire them. Instead Pitroda threw a party. "I'm happy they are going abroad," he said. "They'll take with them all the things they've learned here . . . and if you guys have any problems, you can call them in the United States, and they'll give you answers."

Pitroda recognized that these innovative engineers would eventually move on to new endeavors. He didn't begrudge these departures. He wanted C-DOT to be known as a great laboratory for skill development, a name that would shine brightly on a résumé. Former C-DOT employees are now common in Silicon Valley and fill leadership positions in companies around the world.[11]

Think of a slingshot: it creates forward impetus with a backward pull. For Pitroda's seven employees who wanted to study in the United States, there was an initial step back—a short-term loss of income, the disruption of their professional networks, and moving to a new culture. But in the long term, they saw this as a necessary, temporary backwards move that would help them grow further. And, that's how Pitroda saw it for his organization, too: in the short term, he'd be losing seven very talented employees. A definite step back. But in the long term, by celebrating their success, his organization would become a hub for talent.

Supporting additional education or training is one way of stepping back to grow. In onboarding a new team member or encouraging a person to jump to a new curve, we sacrifice a little near-term productivity. Listening to a curious, clear-eyed, new team member is a step back from our ego.

It's hard to step back. You may be enjoying the exhilarating ride up the steep back of a curve, firing on all cylinders and reaping the payoff of efforts invested at the low end. Why step back now? Or, for that matter, why would an employee be motivated to step back while resting on their laurels at the top of the curve, enjoying a little privilege and entitlement? Because stepping back is your slingshot.

Give Failure Its Due

Not all failures can be sidestepped, nor should they be. Sometimes things break down and we confront the consequences. We may have to let an employee go. If they have been a star performer in the past, it may make sense to reassign them to a different curve. But often failure is the point at which it's important to encourage an employee to try again and keep trying. It may take time for our employees to incorporate and adjust for the feedback they receive. This will require humility on their part, patience on ours. Learning from failure isn't instinctive. But, allow it to be instructive, and it can be a big boost to personal disruption.

Scott Pulsipher knows the sting of failure. He also knows how pivotal a boss can be in using the feedback that comes from failure to create momentum. Soon after business school, he became a VP of product management and marketing at Yantra, a supply chain software startup with $50 million in revenue. When Yantra was acquired by Sterling Commerce (now owned by IBM)—a $450 million company—Pulsipher's responsibilities quickly expanded from managing seven people to managing seventy-five. He was leading vision and strategy, connecting with and influencing people on an individual and a group basis. His executive assistant was also attuned to the needs of others and helped him track and write personal notes weekly. During Pulsipher's tenure, revenue climbed to $600 million while annual employee turnover declined from roughly 18 percent to less than 2 percent. Pulsipher was a boss people loved, because of his people focus.

Fresh off these big wins, Pulsipher joined Amazon, where he reported to Tom Taylor, VP of fulfillment, now senior VP of Alexa. Pulsipher took on the role of GM of a new business called Amazon WebStore. He started in August 2009 and was tasked with launching the venture, which had only pilot customers and zero revenue.

During this high-stakes period, Taylor tapped Pulsipher to attend a leadership training off-site. During one activity, a real-world simulation with twenty-seven high potentials from Amazon, Pulsipher was chosen to receive feedback from every person in the group. They praised him for everything he did that was effective and then told him the truth about everything he wasn't doing well. One criticism hit him like a ton of bricks: while he claimed to be a caring individual, he didn't come across as caring at all when he was tasked with an impossible deadline and high stress. He had become the boss no one wanted to work for.

Pulsipher recalls, "It was rough. Twice I had to stop. It was so emotionally draining, I remember coming home and feeling worthless. Now I realize it was the most meaningful training program I've ever been to. But it wouldn't have worked if Tom Taylor hadn't been there." Taylor pulled him aside: "Sometime between Sterling Commerce and establishing yourself at Amazon, you lost sight of who you are." Under pressure, Pulsipher had become mechanical. Taylor reminded him that he was most effective when his priority was people.

Pulsipher evidently listened to Taylor's good advice. Today, he is president of Western Governors University, one of the largest nonprofit universities in the United States, with more than 85,000 students. One wonders: Would this role have been possible without the punch-in-the-gut of the 360 review, and especially without Tom Taylor encouraging Pulsipher to give failure its due on his path to choosing success?

A manager is a bit like a parent. You push your charges into uncomfortable situations and are willing to see them fail to help them grow and to initiate disruption. At the low end of the curve, this tends to be easier, especially when you hire within the organization. You expect them to flounder. But they have a history of strong performance. So, you (and your boss) can be patient. This gives them the luxury of learning, rather than trying to be loved, allowing them to quickly engage in the actual work.

With employees in the sweet spot of the S curve it can be a bit harder. You may find yourself wanting to shield them from failure. In the short run, this may feel good. In the long run, though, it's riskier to be overprotective. Tasked with undemanding assignments, their confidence begins to falter. They become reluctant to play where others aren't—a hallmark of innovation—and instead of outperforming, they underachieve. Give your employees—especially high potentials—real stretch assignments.[12]

Feyzi (pronounced FAY-zee) Fatehi, CEO of Corent Technology, a cloud and SaaS enablement platform, recounts the experience of a valued and high-performing member of his technical team. We'll call him John. As part of John's career development plan, he asked if he could negotiate and manage a high-stakes strategic partnership. He got what he asked for and pursued it passionately. It didn't work out—in part because he hadn't identified the people who had decision-making authority, but also because John made significant investments without validating his assumptions.

There was a near-term cost to John's misstep. He didn't make his numbers, and there was a resource opportunity cost. But Feyzi leveraged that cost into improving future partnerships as well as into the development of John, a key player, who now, among other lessons learned, identifies decision makers early on. Says Feyzi: "Partly due to John's drive to succeed and our culture of respect and giving each other leeway to experiment, we turned [John's failure] into an investment in his and the company's future."

One possible starting point for giving your team room to make mistakes is to frame expectations for those you report to. For example, if you are a VP reporting up to the C-suite, Stacey Petrey, senior executive compensation consultant at wealth management firm Solenture, suggests the following script: "I can take direction 'XYZ.' There is an 80 percent probability it will work, but there are risks. It is also a stretch assignment for 'so and so.' Win or lose, it's the right risk to take from a business and people development perspective. My team and I will give it our all to succeed, but if we don't, will you back us? Will you support the team and me through this risk?" Most senior leaders forget to frame expectations. "Be honest about the risks," says Petrey, "but also emphasize people development that results from smart risk-taking." Any C-suite executive who is serious about growing their business will sign on.

Encourage Discovery-Driven Growth

In the field of business strategy, discovery-driven planning, made famous by Columbia Business School professor Rita Gunther McGrath, can almost be described as a make-it-up-as-you-go activity.[13] Instead of learning to plan, you plan to learn. Your initial plan is skeletal. It includes questions like, "What would need to happen for this plan to work?" It is then fleshed out as the feedback rolls in, a little at a time.

We can use this approach with managing people, too. For example, to give a promising sales employee time to develop in their position, the sales metric might be, "What can be their minimum sales target for the first six months before we should start to get concerned?" As you learn about that person's capabilities you may periodically redeploy them, improving the match between their strengths and the unmet needs of your team or business. Job descriptions and requirements would be deliberately vague and minimalist rather than rigid. This would help attract talented prospects who can contribute now, while offering potential for roles you haven't yet considered. The data tells us that 70 percent of successful new businesses end up on a course different from the one they initially pursued. Why would it be any different with a person? Flexibility is strength.

It's true that people tend to overlook their innate talents (their superpowers) and instead advertise the skills they've worked hard to acquire. This means that you will occasionally discover you've hired someone onto the wrong S curve. It's not that they don't have the will; it's that they advertised what they do well during the interview process, not what they do best. In such cases, find another S curve for them. If the employee has the skills but not the will, they are similarly on a wrong curve, possibly even in the wrong organization.

As a disruptive manager, you have a purpose, a destination in mind. But how will you get the team there? And what role will each team member play? The story arc is discovered as it is traveled. Quin Snyder, head basketball coach for the NBA's Utah Jazz, manages his players with a discovery-driven approach. During the 2016–2017 basketball season, the team was plagued with injuries, which forced Snyder to constantly reconfigure his five-man lineups. Throughout the first seventy-five of the season's total eighty-two games, he used an incredible twenty-two different starting lineups, figuring out how to optimize his available resources as he went.[14] Snyder emphasizes adaptability in the development of his players. Their ability to move competently from role to role gives them a competitive advantage over teams where players are singularly gifted in just one capacity.

Chatbooks, a Series B–funded startup that helps people create printed scrapbooks from their Instagram photos, also takes a discovery-driven approach to hiring and assigning people to roles within its company. It hires candidates for "high-performance creativity" by seeking qualities such as "grown up," "amazing," "kind," and "optimistic," rather than focusing on pedigree. "Sometimes there's an obvious, long-term fit, sometimes there's not," explains cofounder Vanessa Quigley. "Either way, if they're excited and flexible, we try to hire them, and then they shift into various roles over time. For example, one of our marketing directors took over our email campaigns for six months while we searched for someone to do that job. Now she's spearheading a new content initiative. Our business development director came on to lead a product extension, but we found that we wanted to use her skills for chasing new deals. We are willing to shift people into new roles so that the business needs—and their passions—align." Chatbooks' model of matching S-curve development with changing business needs has served the company well. It has printed hundreds of millions of photos and millions of books and tripled revenue for each of the last three years.[15]

The discovery-driven approach lets you decide what you want to accomplish (growing equity returns by 15 percent per year, for example), then figure out who can make it happen. Who can incur the cost (the skill and the will) to achieve your goal? What are your assumptions about the contribution each team member can make? Create a milestone chart so you know if people are on track one month in, three months in, etc. If needed, course correct. As a discovery-driven manager, you are continually load-balancing your team, optimizing for the different phases with skills and will as the found-ation. Pit people against real challenges—and innovation will follow.

Summary

Managers need to know about seven accelerants of learning. These include:

1. THE RIGHT RISKS: Become a talent developer.

2. DISTINCTIVE STRENGTHS: Pinpoint employees' talents and utilize them.

3. EMBRACE CONSTRAINTS: Use time limits to motivate and hone focus.

4. BATTLE AGAINST ENTITLEMENT: Celebrate success, and be generous in helping employees fulfill their potential.

5. STEP BACK TO GROW: Sacrifice short-term productivity to encourage curve jumping.

6. GIVE FAILURE ITS DUE: Let employees take on uncomfortable challenges, and support them through failures.

7. BE DISCOVERY DRIVEN: Shift players on your team as their skills and talents emerge.

RECRUITING AND HIRING

A company is a living, breathing entity. It is either evolving or dying.

—**Angela Blanchard**

Butte, Montana, began to attract miners during the mid-nineteenth century, primarily to pan and dig for gold and silver. There were some successes, but Butte didn't live up to the expectations elevated by its early gold rush. Despite this, it is still referred to as "the richest hill on earth." Why?

Within a few decades of the initial rush, disappointed speculators were selling their mining claims in Butte for dirt cheap. A handful of people began to buy up and consolidate claims and mining operations, content to extract wealth at a more leisurely pace than the earliest settlers had hoped for. Importantly, they began to discover and exploit copper—a low-end resource at the time. The development of several technologies, principally electrical wiring, made copper valuable—extremely valuable.

The few who by then held most of the property and mineral rights became some of the wealthiest people in the world as they reaped the windfall of discovery-driven resource exploration and development. They are collectively referred to as the Copper Kings. Butte presented a once-in-a-lifetime opportunity, but that potential wasn't recognized by the gold seekers with their dreams of instant gratification.

I often think of the story of Butte when managers tell me they can't find qualified candidates, complain that schools don't turn out graduates with the right skills, or that they have an opening that's just impossible to fill. Really?

Think of a role that is currently open in your company or on your team. What are the requisite capabilities? Are these the minimum competencies required, or are you stuck in the rut of expecting top-of-the-curve expertise? Are you seeking the gold standard? Or will silver do? How about copper? There are compelling reasons to go for copper.

Humans as Resources

Here's what usually sets the stage for a new hire: we're shorthanded and overwhelmed. A key employee has moved within the company, opted for a fresh start elsewhere, or taken a leave of absence. Maybe business has suddenly ramped up with the signing of a new client or the winning of a large contract. We need help in the form of a body who can step into the role today and do the job now. Someone to salve our pain.

Desperate, we hire the person who we perceive to be the most qualified to fill the void, and for a time, they do. "Marry in haste, repent at leisure," goes the adage. Because we hired someone at the top of the curve, within months they are bored and looking around for a new suitor. Soon we'll be back at square one: overwhelmed, on the rebound, and poised to hire in haste again.

That's not a great use of resources. Utilizing resources profitably begins with recognizing potential, followed by a period of exploration, discovery, and development. This is how we learn what works and what does not; this is how we uncover what is possible. When we think of people, truly, as human *resources*, rather than expecting them to be ready-made products, we follow a similar approach. Hiring for potential rather than proficiency is the foundation for building an A-team.

I recognize that this approach is antithetical to some HR practices. Think about the last job requisition you posted. You probably tried to hire someone at the top of the learning curve who already knew how to do everything the job required—plus the kitchen sink. It's natural for busy managers to think to themselves, "I don't have time to train someone; we need someone who can do the job on day one." Moreover, managers often have an incentive to write inflated job descriptions, because in many organizations doing so makes it more likely that their request for a new hire will be approved ("Look how much this new hire will do!"), and when it is approved, it gives them more of a salary budget to play with.

There are downsides to hiring this way. One is that the "wish list" approach to job qualifications turns off many employees who don't fit the bill. Some studies suggest that women especially are less likely to apply for jobs they're not 100 percent qualified for, under the mistaken impression that job requirements are actually, well, "requirements."[1]

Another downside is that when we recruit by advertising for maximum rather than minimum qualifications and hire the most qualified candidate in the applicant pool, we have already shortened their shelf life. With little room to rise, the new hire will be feeling stale in no time. While they acclimate to a new culture, their lack of challenge likely won't immediately be obvious, but after a few months they will be predictably bored.

We will then either find a new role for them to fill, or they will leave (more than 40 percent of employees who voluntarily leave their jobs do so within six months of their start date, and half have moved on in less than a year).[2] Considering the cost of recruitment and hiring and the investment required in initial training, this is a mind-boggling waste of resources.

In 2005, Eileen Appelbaum, senior economist at the Center for Economic and Policy Research, and her colleague Ruth Milkman, professor of sociology at CUNY (City University of New York), conducted case studies on thirteen employers in New Jersey in which they broke down turnover costs for both hourly employees and salaried managerial and professional employees.[3] They examined often-overlooked costs such as the salary of recruiters, the cost per hour to conduct interviews with two or three salaried managers, the cost of the employee's time who is training a new hire, advertising fees, travel related to recruitment and interviewing, time spent on screening and background checks, and many other costs of turnover.

Their research led to the creation of an interactive employee turnover calculator to help businesses break down the cost of hiring a new employee. What they found is eye-opening.[4] The cost to replace an employee in the United States earning $75,000 or less (which accounts for a high percentage of total employees) is about 20 percent of the employee's annual salary. Those costs increase dramatically for highly compensated senior executives and employees with highly specialized skills, topping 200 percent of their annual salary.[5] Losing employees costs businesses thousands, even hundreds of thousands of dollars. Get recruiting and hiring right, and you impact the bottom line.

Meredith Kopit Levien, executive VP and COO of the *New York Times*, names *Forbes* CEO Mike Perlis as her most influential boss. Why? Because when he promoted her to chief revenue officer at *Forbes*, she was not an expert in digital media—she was at the low end of this curve. There were many naysayers who wondered, "How the hell is she going to do this job? She's a magazine publisher." But she describes Perlis as having "unbelievable patience" and a belief in her, which gave her confidence. "He gave me the space to . . . figure it out," she says. Meredith was in this role for five years before she was hired away by the *New York Times*. That's retention.

Patrick Pichette, former CFO of Google, was at the top of his curve when he was recruited into Google—but his boss understood that even C-level employees need the thrill of learning. "The job was not what I wanted at all," he said. He had already been a CFO at two previous firms. However, in his meeting with Google CEO Eric Schmidt, Pichette reports that Schmidt was very savvy. He remembers Schmidt saying, "Well, we have a real problem, Patrick. After eighteen months, you'll be totally bored and you're going to go and do something else. I'll tell you what: I'll hire you as CFO, and we'll give you this and that and the other to start with, and every time it looks like you are about to lose interest, I'm going to add stuff onto your plate."[6] Schmidt made good on his offer. "That's how I ended up over time with finance, organization, the people operations, the real estate, all the employee services, Google Fiber, Google.org," Pichette relates. He spent seven years with Google before taking a sabbatical to travel and engage in environmental and other philanthropic causes.

The motivation for adopting an S curve management strategy is recognition that time plus competence equals boredom. Unless new variables are added to the equation, boredom quickly becomes synonymous with low engagement and declining productivity. The key to building a high-functioning team begins with a deliberate recruitment process: hire at the low end of the S curve.

Hire People Who Can Grow on the Job

Begin by reminding yourself that the goal is to approach human resources as raw materials rather than as finished products, the same way you would handle other resources. The following list constitutes the phase of exploration:

1. Identify the tasks you want a new hire to perform.

2. Do a team check: consider how the new role will affect the team.

3. Do a sanity check: identify your motivation for the new hire.

4. Write a job post to attract the ideal person.

Identify the Tasks You Want a New Hire to Perform

First, identify *what* you need done.

An empty space on the roster can put extreme pressure on your team, and their pain quickly becomes yours. Hiring someone just to make the pain go away is a powerful urge but a poor idea. Optimal hiring requires time and thought both to map and execute.

Start with the question: What is my need? The obvious response is, "I need a (fill-in-the-blank [systems, payroll, marketing, finance]) person." This is a simple variable in the hiring equation, but we don't always do a good job of solving for it. Rather than really thinking about what we want done, we usually assume we need someone to do what the previous employee in the role did, particularly if that person performed their part well. If we're lucky, a great candidate will come along and tell us what we really need.

Five years ago, Michelle McKenna-Doyle (who you met in chapter 2) was at a crossroads in her career. The company she worked for was going through a merger, and to retain her position as CIO, she would have to relocate, which she didn't want to do. A devoted sports fan, McKenna-Doyle happened to be on the NFL website picking her fantasy football team when she noticed a link for jobs, which led her to a job opening for a VP of IT (information technology). Not knowing anyone at the NFL, McKenna-Doyle started combing her network to come up with someone who could make a warm introduction. It turned out that was the easy part. When I spoke with her she said, "When I read the description, I thought, 'They need a CIO, not a VP of IT.' They need to upgrade the position—make it a CIO, make it a senior vice president, give this role a seat at the table."

Roger Goodell, commissioner of the NFL, got McKenna-Doyle's vision: how she would connect the dots among the NFL's divisions from a technology and information perspective. She recalls Goodell telling her, "You've sold me. I've sold our CFO and HR. Now, you've got to sell it to everybody else. No one here is going to know what a CIO is; we've never had one of you before." It took some time to convince the NFL to expand her role beyond managing the data center and keeping the phones up and running. But by the time she finished her first year there, McKenna-Doyle had implemented so many valuable initiatives that there was no question the CIO role was and is vital to the future of her organization.

Hers is a great dream-job-come-true story. It also illustrates a common hiring mistake: the NFL advertised a job opening for a VP of IT because that was the job title of the person who had left.

When you have a job opening on your team, instead of habitually posting openings using recycled job descriptions from previous hiring cycles, evaluate what you need now. Don't accept that it has to stay as it currently is. Genuinely understand what you are looking for, then make the effort to find it. Rather than requiring the ideal candidate to possess mastery of the entire skill set for the job, hire people for their low-end-of-the-curve *capacity* to fill many roles, not just the top-shelf, high-end-of-the-curve *qualifications* for one role. What are the minimum, rather than the maximum, competencies required to be successful? Think copper, not gold.

Remember to include soft skills. What are some of the less-tangible qualities that would benefit the team? Which ones make an individual a good fit with your company culture? Are some of these less-tangible abilities noticeably missing in the current composition of the team? Are you in need of a good organizer? Someone who writes well or is adept with the public? A peacemaker, challenger, or facilitator? Someone creative with a lot of technical expertise who is also comfortable with people?

Most candidates for a job come with a body of acquired knowledge and skills. These things will be listed on their résumé and emphasized in the cover letter. These individuals also have strengths, or "superpowers": things they do instinctively that may not be clearly articulated in their job application. By identifying some of the human qualities that we value in a hire, we make it easier to read between the lines to discern them; we can prepare to probe for them during the interview process. This is where references can be helpful. Let's always be open to superpowers, even if we haven't identified a pressing need for them. Superpowers are where an individual's greatest potential lies.

There's a lot of literature on CEO succession and the cross-disciplinary experience deemed necessary.[7] The fact is, every hire is important. You are trying to fill both an individual contributor pipeline and a leadership one with promising talent. Investment in ahead-of-the-curve exploration will be repaid with the discovery of better raw material. Be strategic with your hires—every one of them.

Consider How a New Role Will Affect the Team

What percentage of team members are currently at the low end of their S curves? Do you have 15 percent at the low end, 70 percent in the middle, and 15 percent at the high end? While I generally argue for hiring people at the low end of the learning curve so they have runway, if you're managing a team of novices it might make sense to hire (or rent) someone more seasoned.

Now look back at the list of skills and qualifications you've listed for this new role. Are there tasks other members of your team could take on as development opportunities? When we see the same people at work every day they can become like wallpaper: we no longer focus on their specific work as well as we ought to. With a little effort, we may discover that we have an employee near or at the top of their current learning curve who is perfectly poised to jump to the low end of the S curve we were thinking of hiring for. Making an internal hire often means we've created the potential for at least two employees to grow: the one we've promoted and the one we're hiring.

Also, understand how your people work together. How might a new hire enhance the capacities your team already has? Are you short a soprano or a tenor? Missing an accompanist? Is there a soloist in the choir, and is their contribution harmonious or does it grate on the ear despite the quality of their voice? Where are the gaps in good team coordination and compatibility?

When Dave Winsborough, VP of innovation at Hogan Assessments, was only twelve, a couple of classmates beat him up for always knowing the answers and outperforming his scholastic peers.[8] He credits this experience with kindling a lifelong fascination with group dynamics. Winsborough has collaborated with Tomas Chamorro-Premuzic,

Hogan Assessment's CEO, to synthesize the results of varied research around teaming. They state:

> A useful way to think about teams . . . is to consider the two roles every person plays in a working group: a *functional* role, based on their formal position and technical skill, and a *psychological* role, based on the kind of person they are. Some employees feel an almost zealous sense of mission about their work; others embrace it as valuable to varying degrees but without a sense of personal calling. These differences in sentiment can be points of contention. Too often, organizations focus merely on the functional role and hope that good team performance somehow follows.[9]

To further plumb the psychological aspect, you may want to administer the Disruptive Strengths Indicator (DSI). This tool (available at whitneyjohnson.com/diagnostic) examines which of the seven accelerants of learning and growth (outlined in chapter 2) people rely on to manage through change. Are they especially good at playing to their strengths, embracing constraints, or rebounding from failure? You can work through this assessment for the individual and then perform the same evaluation on the team.

Team dysfunction is like family dysfunction: it undermines individual development and is counterproductive to the purposes of the whole. Envision employee roles as sinuous S curves weaving together to form a whole cloth of great strength. Excessive friction is a barrier to progress that can hold or even push people down the curve. If you view your employees as discrete threads with little synergistic interaction, your team will fray instead of becoming a fine piece of fabric. Get the relationships right and the sum of your team will be greater than its parts.

Identify Your Motivation for the Hire

Research on consumer behavior demonstrates that we tend to buy the same things time and again, virtually without thought. A.G. Lafley, two-time CEO at Procter & Gamble, and Roger L. Martin examined these results while investigating why frequent rebranding—going for a "new look"—doesn't necessarily translate into a competitive advantage. They found that in fact customers have a reflexive preference for the tried-and-true, thus leading familiar brands to a compounding competitive advantage over time. They conclude: "Research into the workings of the human brain suggests that the mind loves automaticity more than just about anything else—certainly more than engaging in conscious consideration. Given a choice, it would like to do the same things over and over."[10]

As a manager performing a hiring function, you are a consumer of talent, susceptible to the tendency to constantly and thoughtlessly repeat your consumption habits. While this may not matter much when choosing laundry detergent, it can have dire consequences when hiring. Circumstances change, needs may evolve over time, or earlier iterations of the job description may have been poorly thought out.

The prior team member may have been competent but didn't always bring what we ideally wanted to the table, or maybe they didn't play with the team as cooperatively as we would have liked, and so on. Hiring is the optimal time to address these issues.

Underlying our conscious exploration and evaluation, each of us also has a subconscious mind at work, potentially influencing our decision making—and not always for the better. Before making your final choices about whether and how to hire, do a "sanity check" to bring your subconscious and emotional motivations to the surface for examination as well. Essentially, we want to identify how we are hoping to "feel better" because of a new hire. What pain points do we hope to eliminate? Having identified these, we may require an adjustment to our expectations. If we onboard someone who can do the functional job but can't do the emotional job, we won't be satisfied no matter what they do.[11] Precipitous hiring may leave us with unmet functional needs as well.

Here are some of the subconscious emotional motivations that we rarely address head on but that we would do well to consider:

1. If only I could clone myself. According to Lauren Rivera, associate professor of management and organizations and sociology at Northwestern University's Kellogg School of Management, "What most people are looking for is 'me.'" Her studies suggest that "interviewers who lacked systematic measures of what their company was looking for tended to fall back on themselves and defined merit in 'their own image,' meaning that the most-qualified interviewees were those who best resembled their interviewers."[12] Rivera became interested in examining hiring practices after observing the recruiting efforts of elite professional service firms, first as an undergraduate at Yale being recruited and later working for a recruiting firm. "I've always been fascinated by social status and how people judge merit," she says. "Hiring is one of the most consequential status sorts that people experience, and I wanted to know more about how employers evaluate and select new hires. Hiring in these [professional service] firms matters not just for individuals' own salaries or careers, but also for the composition of the American economic elite more broadly."[13]

It's easy to want to make this kind of hire: a carbon copy of yourself. Someone who thinks like you do and is readily agreeable to your approach. But they will be bored and frustrated quickly because there's no headroom. You already have you. It's also possible that you will feel threatened by this shinier version of you. It's uncomfortable to have someone crowding you out on your S curve.

If you're thinking about hiring a clone of yourself, you're not thinking about S curves. Nor have you identified a discrete role for this new hire. Instead, view the pressure you're feeling to hire as an opportunity to do something differently than before, to innovate. Maybe you delegate more, offering team members new mountains to climb. Perhaps you make better use of technology. Once you start considering options, you'll realize how many good ones there are.

2. If only I could find someone to do all the annoying stuff I don't want to do.
This mentality comes from a desire to avoid all the disagreeable parts of your job or to find a scapegoat for everyone to hate so that you can be loved. A few years ago, I was invited to interview for the position of CFO at a fast-growing tech company. There are a lot of roles a CFO can play, but when the COO said to me, "I'm looking for someone to tell everyone how much they can't spend," my sense was he was hoping to outsource the job of financial henchman. If you want to offload everything that you detest doing to a new hire, it's likely they'll also become your emotional dumping ground and you won't like them (a sentiment they will be inclined to return). Nor will you be motivated to invest in them. When this person reaches the top of their S curve—if they stay that long—you won't care enough to help them jump to a new one.

If you think this way when hiring, you will have retention problems. Just as looking for a clone may mean you need to delegate more, wanting a "bad cop" may mean it's time to take on more of the grunt work yourself. At the very least, learn to discern between delegating tasks that will optimize your team's performance and a penchant for off-loading tasks that are your responsibility.

3. If only I knew how to do that.   There may be tasks that demand attention that you don't personally have the expertise to complete. It's why you are hiring someone. But sometimes there is an undercurrent of envy, a secret longing. *If I knew how to do what they know how to do, I'd be more successful.*

You may hope to live vicariously through a capable person, possibly enjoy advancement on the strength of their abilities. Or you may feel threatened because they have talents you lack. Either way, you risk overpaying financially—and emotionally.

Instead of taking this approach, couch the emotion this way: *If only I knew what I don't know.* Don't just say it, learn to really mean it. Simple reason requires that we accept that we have limitations and acknowledge what they are—even that we search them out, if we've been avoiding the fact of their existence. If you really want to move your organization forward, hire people with varied skill sets and who are seeking different S curves. Find people who disagree with you. Open your team to those who aren't like you, who challenge your thinking, and who will point out what you don't know.

To the extent you lack mastery over areas of the domain you manage, part of your S curve is to learn. Amanda Goodall, senior lecturer at Cass Business School in London, has spent her career exploring the relationship between leadership domain expertise and employee engagement and longevity. She asserts that "the benefit of having a highly competent boss is easily the largest positive influence on a typical worker's level of job satisfaction . . . Among American workers, having a technically competent boss is considerably more important for employee job satisfaction than their salary (even when pay is really high)."[14] Significantly, Goodall has replicated her research multiple times across various sectors with the same results: doctors are happier when hospital administrators are also doctors, professional athletes are more satisfied when coaches and managers are former players, academics prefer other academics as university administrators, and so on. If this is you, remember that your employees don't want you to do their job for them, even though you could. But they do work better knowing that you understand what they do.

Let go of expertise envy. Hire people who know what you don't. But know enough that you comprehend the challenges you ask them to tackle, can value their good work, and help them onto curves that will maximize their talent.

Write a Job Post to Attract the Ideal Person

Writing job postings is more of an art form than most of us realize. A friend of mine was feeling a bit stagnant in her role: she'd been with the same company for ten years and in the same job for the past three. While she loved her company, she was ready for a new learning curve. So she was browsing the job postings in her industry just to see what other options might be out there. She was becoming quite discouraged, reading description after description that sounded tedious and uncreative, when she suddenly happened upon a job opening in her own company. She'd known the woman who'd worked in that role—it was a fabulous job. But the description was just as bad as all the others. Suddenly and counterintuitively, she was full of hope. If her own company, where she'd loved working for the past decade, could post such a repellent job description for such a fantastic role, then maybe those other jobs being advertised weren't so bad either. Just think how powerfully a great job listing would stand out in such a landscape.

The goal of a job posting should be to attract talented people who are qualified to onboard at the *low end* of the job's learning curve. They won't be experts, but they will have what it takes to learn and magnify their current position and other roles beyond it. Catching the eye of these candidates requires a change in how job requirements are typically articulated. Dorothy Dalton, an international talent management strategist, concurs:

> For the hiring manager, the seniority and level of a team can be an in-house status symbol. On some occasions the academic requirements demanded for some positions would ordinarily be sufficient to split the atom or find a cure for cancer. MBAs are not essential for all openings. If we are honest, many jobs don't even require a degree, let alone any post-grad qualifications. Provided literacy, numeracy, and social skills are in place as well as any relevant professional experience, the university of life would be just fine . . . The same can be said for years and type of experience required.[15]

If we inflate the necessary qualifications, focus on high-end-of-the-curve capacity, and then hire the applicant who comes closest to meeting these criteria, we set the stage for a poor employment fit. Instead, we need to temper our overblown ambitions and look for a quality, high-potential candidate who won't become disinterested within the first few months of employment. Write the job posting to encourage, rather than deter, such applicants.

There is a considerable body of literature available to assist in striking the right tone in our job postings. Gender neutrality in language, for instance, is critical.[16] In most cases this is necessary to encourage women to apply, but not always. In many medical professions traditionally occupied by women, for example, studies show that men are discouraged from applying because the language of job advertisements is perceived as too feminine.[17] Encouraging diversity in the applicant pool is a necessary step to fostering diversity in the workplace. Pamela Rice, head of technology strategy at Capital One, has a strong track record for hiring diverse candidates. "There is a knock-on effect that occurs when organizations invest in diversity," she explains. "They automatically see more diverse candidates being referred, and diverse candidates flock to companies where their impact is recognized and appreciated. It's also no surprise that the innovation and products coming out of these diverse teams are more compelling to users who happen to be diverse as well."

Make it clear in the job posting why this role really matters. A nationwide survey by Net Impact and Rutgers University, for example, reveals that "employees who say they can make an impact while on the job report greater satisfaction than those who can't by a 2:1 ratio. This data is backed up by the two-thirds of graduating university students who tell us that making a difference through their next job is a priority and 45 percent of students say they would even take a pay cut to do so."[18] In fact, 58 percent of the surveyed workers of all ages claimed they would accept a 15 percent loss in basic compensation to work for a company with values aligned to their own. While there are gender differences reported, with values-oriented work being somewhat more important to women than men, and slight differences across generations, the data points overwhelmingly to a workforce that is hungry to perform tasks that matter.

We want to contribute and feel energized, even passionate about what we do. We want to be inspired by ideas that can solve problems. For most, the meaning of the work doesn't have to matter in the broadest sense. We don't insist on changing the world or addressing cosmically important issues. But we do yearn to believe that we are making our corner of the world happier in some small but significant way. Make the case that the S curve you are hiring for matters; convey this sense of consequence through the job description.

Hire Where Others Aren't

When hiring managers say they can't find anyone for a role, I always wonder if they've looked at internal candidates, caregivers returning to the workforce, or military veterans. There's really *no one* out there for your open job?

This goes back to the concept of market risk and competitive risk described in chapter 2. Sure, there's some risk in hiring a nontraditional candidate—but it's market risk, because you're playing in a green field with few competitors. Hiring an Ivy League–educated MBA who has

What to Focus On in the Interview

Here's a summary of what you want to learn about potential candidates during the application vetting and interview process.

- Functionally, where does this person fit on the envisioned S curve? Soft skills are as important as domain expertise.

- How comfortable is the candidate with personal disruption, with playing the game of chutes and ladders? And which of the seven accelerants of personal disruption do they rely on to manage change? The DSI (Disruptive Strengths Indicator) diagnostic can help with this evaluation.

- How do they team? How does their temperament match with what you need? Administering a diagnostic test before hiring may be useful.

done the exact job you need doing for the past three years might feel safe, but it's actually a form of competitive risk. You'll be competing with a dozen other rival firms for that candidate.

Hiring where others aren't begins with internal hiring: promoting or moving people who want to try something new. They are frequently at the top of one S curve. What

- What are their broader purposes and dreams? How does what they care about fit with the objectives articulated for your team or business?

- Invite questions. A lot can be gleaned from the effort a candidate has put into their own research and exploration about the opportunity. Have they thoroughly investigated the organization? Do they ask thoughtful questions about the role they might be brought in to fill? In their mind, is this the job that needs to be done? Is their interest limited to information about the compensation package and vacation time—and do they exhibit enthusiasm about the value of the work or the quality of the growth and learning opportunities? Attention given to these nuances during the interview process will pay off.

they propose to do next may be considered a step back in terms of title and even compensation. Ultimately, titles and compensation are subjective designations. They can be adapted to reflect opportunity and contribution rather than being tied solely to outmoded hierarchical models. Proven employees who jump at something different, despite the disadvantages, are a hugely overlooked resource.

Also consider unconventional hiring arrangements. While data varies greatly from survey to survey, there are reports that in 2016, 30 percent or more of workers performed some contract or freelance work.[19] Some of these workers want to be permanent participants in the gig economy, but not all. Firms sometimes hire on a contract or freelance basis to see if there is a fit. Many of these firms have a pathway for interns, freelancers, and contract workers to become full-time employees.

Once such a pathway is in place it can also be applied to the hiring of nontraditional employees: "on-rampers (those who have taken a break from the full-time career highway but are now ready to return), nondegreed workers, returning military personnel, and retirees," says iRelaunch cofounder Carol Fishman Cohen. An advocate for the value of the unconventional labor pool, she provides guidelines for how employers can implement mid-career internship programs and access the return-to-work pool. She also has compelling data to share: for example, MetLife hired eleven out of twelve (92 percent) of its mid-career interns after about three months.[20]

One group of nontraditional employees to pay particular attention to is on-rampers. Many of these are women who've been caring for children. The Center for Work-Life Policy found that 69 percent of highly qualified women—those with an advanced university degree or very prestigious undergraduate degree at a minimum—report that they would have stayed in the workforce all along if their employer could have arranged a more flexible situation for them, while 89 percent of these women would like to return to work, usually within just a few years.[21]

It isn't only women. Men also choose to take career breaks for a variety of reasons: child care, elder care, a period of ill health, additional education, and more. After a decade at home as lead parent, my husband was ready to go back to work.[22] He's a cancer researcher with a doctorate degree from Columbia University who was formerly an assistant professor at UMass Medical School. When he launched his effort to on-ramp, no one was interested, in spite of his credentials. Eventually an associate vouched for him with Southern Virginia University, a small liberal arts college in central Virginia. He's now back on the tenure track, something that rarely happens when a person takes a break from academia. He's entirely focused on teaching and has an entrepreneurial streak that fits well with the goals of this ambitious and expanding school. It's a win-win. The position is a new curve for him and the university gets a highly engaged employee—all because they were willing to hire him when others were not.

On-rampers are especially attractive because they often possess the skills that the workplace needs. Think of the competencies required to care for family, either parents or children. These skills are often in high demand and short supply. Michelle R. Weise, senior VP of workforce strategies and chief innovation officer at Strada Education Network, summarizes research by Burning Glass Technologies that identifies the qualifications almost universally desired by employers, regardless of sector or specialty: presentation and persuasion; customer service; attention to detail and time management;

positive disposition; project management, research, and strategy; and supervisory skills. These are all abilities honed by effective parents and providers of elder care.[23]

David Blake, founder of learning platform Degreed, puts it more succinctly: "Degrees suck!" His company promotes the idea that degrees signify only a small percentage of a person's actual education. So Blake is innovating ways for individuals to map—and for potential employers to verify—the full landscape of education and skills, however they are acquired.[24]

At IBM's Rocket Center in West Virginia, where the focus is on cloud computing, cybersecurity, application development, and help desks, nearly a third of new hires in the past two years have not had four-year college degrees. Sean Bridges is one of these unconventional hires. He came to IBM with no work history, but he had certain demonstrable skills. He had studied information technology at a community college, and he had built and sold some stripped-down personal computers. Bridges is now a computer security analyst for IBM. He represents a new category in the labor market: "new collar" or middle-skill jobs, where skills (such as coding) are more important than pedigree (college degrees and job history).[25] In the United States, where two-thirds of adults do not have a four-year college degree, finding candidates to fill roles may require taking a chance on unconventional hires.[26] Potential is manifest not only—and perhaps not best—in conventional credentials.

Then there's the boomerang employee: someone who has worked at the organization in the past. Once it was common to have a policy against rehiring former employees, but fortunately more companies are doing away with such rules. Skills acquired in a different venue can make a former employee even more valuable. Lee Caraher, author of *The Boomerang Principle: Inspire Lifetime Loyalty from Your Employees*, says, "Stop thinking about job hoppers as lost employees. Treat people well and help them realize their goals, wherever this may take them, and the person you felt left too soon might hop right back to you and be even more valuable the second time."

Caraher's company, Double Forte, practices what she preaches. The PR, content marketing, and social media firm has had over a dozen employees boomerang, some of them twice. Jenna Galloway Faller had been at Double Forte for two years as a senior account executive when she left for a dream position with a VC-backed fast-casual food startup. Faller left with Double Forte's assurance that the door was open if she wanted to return. A year later, she did, with enhanced skills in PR management, a greater empathy for Double Forte's traditional customers and, as she says, "a new appreciation for this industry and our company's culture, making me a very enthusiastic employee and manager."

We may be inclined to pass over nontraditional candidates because we think they are defective in some way. We may be fearful of making a mistake and allow risk aversion to triumph in our decision making. But market risk is where the big opportunity awaits. Coss Marte is a former drug dealer who ran a very lucrative business until he went to prison. Now he is a legitimate CEO operating a Manhattan-based health club, ConBody, that employs the formerly incarcerated as fitness instructors and personal trainers. This is an extreme example of hiring where others won't—and it is proving to be a great success.

Nontraditional employees can be storehouses of education, skill, and experience that you can put to work. They have S curves too, and other employers' absence of vision can be your gain. When you hire where others aren't, the options aren't picked over. They're not overpriced. The candidates are often hungry and have something to prove.

As with the copper in Butte, Montana, raw materials of great value are found in unlikely places and may often be overlooked. Today, smartphones contain sixteen of the seventeen rare-earth metals, resources that were left behind in the waste rock of mining ventures until the advent of sophisticated electronics.[27] These elements are referred to as "rare" not because they are scarce (although a few of them are) but because they are dispersed throughout the earth's crust, rather than concentrated in any one place. They may literally be found right under our feet, but they require unconventional methods to extract them. Valuable human resources are like this: if we are willing to be unconventional in our recruiting and hiring, we can discover and develop them. Seeking out what has been overlooked is the bedrock of innovation.

Summary

- Recruiting and hiring for an S curve strategy requires overhauling traditional practices. Conscious evaluation of functional capacity as well as desirable soft skills is essential. Also be sure to evaluate any emotional expectations that you may have attached to the new hire.

- Hire people who are willing to try new things and who aren't afraid to start at the bottom of the S curve. Bring in managers who can spot talent, can help people move up the curve to mastery, and who are willing to sponsor and facilitate jumps to new curves.

- Look for expansive potential rather than proficiency. When we hire the "most qualified" candidate, we are choosing to shorten the period of high engagement. Plan to hire new recruits—or reassignments—at the low end of the S curve and to invest in their development as a resource.

- In addition to evaluating each position before recruiting and hiring, evaluate how your team is functioning before bringing in a new player.

- Recruiting from unconventional talent pools and hiring specifically for an S curve strategy means embracing market risk: playing where other employers disdain to play. This is where the greatest opportunity for a real win is found.

- Focus on long-term resource development. Evaluate for aptitude and willingness to engage in personal disruption. Craft job postings to encourage a wide range of people to apply.

MANAGING THE HUNGRY NEW HIRE

A man who carries a cat by the tail learns
something he can learn in no other way.

—Mark Twain

John Gooch was ready for a change. In his mid-fifties, after fifteen years of running his own civil engineering and soil-testing business, he and his partners decided to sell their assets, and Gooch went to work for a nonprofit. When he discovered the new job wasn't a good fit, he mentioned this to long-time professional friend, Don Cantore, the CEO of Fielder's Choice Enterprises, an excavating firm specializing in large infrastructure projects. Cantore didn't know of any available jobs, but after thinking about it overnight, he decided he'd like to hire Gooch. Cantore offered him a job as a junior estimator. He couldn't pay Gooch what he was used to, but he could offer a decent salary and get him trained in a year or two.

This would be a big step back for Gooch, both economically and in terms of expertise, especially so late in his career. Gooch had transferable skills as an engineer but hadn't done much estimating, nor did he have experience with large-scale infrastructure, like building bridges. The learning curve was steep, and he had sleepless nights for eight to ten months at the start. Now, with three years under his belt, he is no longer junior but a regular estimator. He says there is much still to learn, but the company has been great. A "really good group of people" have made it possible for him to successfully make this career pivot.[1]

The low end of the S curve is usually occupied by early-career new hires or talented professionals with deep domain expertise who are branching out. You optimize your team with 15 percent of your people at the low end. This chapter will explain how to successfully onboard these new hires, which includes outlining the why of your organization and team, understanding your new hire's goals, and articulating your vision of what they can accomplish in this role. We will discuss how to manage the first six months, using constraints for quick feedback. We will also help you embrace a short-term loss of productivity while discussing the unique qualities and compensating advantages that ambitious S curve low-enders bring to the table. And finally, we will provide a checklist for determining if progress is slow because your new employee is on the wrong curve or simply at the low end.

Successfully Onboarding Your New Hire

As you set out to manage your recent hire, there are a few things to consider. First, how to communicate your vision—or the "why" of the organization. Second, you'll want to understand your employee's "why" (e.g., why they came to work for you). Third, you must have vision for your new employee—how you'd like them to develop, and how you will gauge if they are succeeding in their new role.

Communicate Your Vision—the "Why" of the Organization and Your Team

When our son was in high school, at least once a week he would say, "What is the point of school? I am never going to use [insert subject] again." The counterargument was, "You may not use all of it. But good grades get you into college, and knowing how to work gets you into a happy life." On days when I was desperate or just exasperated, I would huff, "Do it because I said to." I would often lament to my husband, "Why doesn't he have a vision for his future?" In trying to understand why teenagers procrastinate, psychologist Timothy Pychyl discovered that "until we have a vision of who we want to become, we can't do much." Once we have a vision, we get stuff done.

New hires need a vision. Understanding why their job is necessary and important will power them through difficult days, when the cost of the struggle toward competence seems steep. For the first three to six months on the job, they may struggle with discouragement. They may try your patience. You may even wonder why you hired them. And maybe it *was* a bad hire; it's too soon to know. But you can increase their odds of moving up the learning curve by laying out a vision from the outset.

Start with the why of your organization—and your team. You may be reluctant to do so. There are too many things clamoring for your attention. You need your new hire to get right to work. (One benefit of hiring internally is that the new hire will already have an idea of what the company is about.)

Maybe you feel that you can't offer a clear vision. After all, doesn't the word "vision" imply the ability to see the path ahead and chart your course accordingly? As a discovery-driven disruptor, you may not see exactly where you're going. But even if you don't know what lies ahead, chances are you know *why* you are moving in that direction. The purpose that drives what you are doing is foundational. It is worth the time to examine, understand, and share it with your team.

One company that articulates its vision from the get-go is Globalization Partners (GP) in Cambridge, Massachusetts, which in 2017 was ranked number 33 on *Inc.* magazine's prestigious Inc. 5000, an annual list of the fastest-growing private companies in the United States.[2] Week one on the job, each employee goes through GP University. The first day they spend time with CEO Nicole Sahin, who explains her vision for the company: "Venture capital, private equity, and public companies only consider their shareholders, thus maximizing profit on a quarterly basis at a cost to the well-being of clients and employees." Sahin defines success as "A triple bottom line: happy employees equals happy clients equals happy shareholders." The employees then hear presentations from every director in the company. This sets the stage for cross-silo collaboration and respect, quashing entitlement from the start. Not surprisingly, people like to work there. In a survey done by CultureIQ, GP received a 92 out of 100 in its employee net promoter score, a barometer of employee loyalty. And job-search company Glassdoor, which amasses worker reviews, indicates that most current and past employees give GP solid reviews.

There are endless methods and tactics, but there are very few "whys." When we have a vision and believe in it, instead of seeing drudgery, we see discovery. Instead of aimless wandering, we see ourselves on a defined path to proficiency, at the low end of our personal growth curve. Once there is a why, there is a way.

Understand Your New Hire's Vision—Their "Why"

Just as your new employee needs to understand the company's vision, you'll want to understand theirs. Find out what they are trying to accomplish as a person and how this new role fits with their goals, as well as what they anticipate they will need from you to be successful. Ideally, in the first week of employment, you'll hold a strategy session with your employee, just as you would with a customer. In fact, a new hire *is* a customer: a highly important, long-term customer.

(For more on this, see the sidebar "The New Hire: The First Week.")

There's both risk and responsibility associated with asking these questions. Knowledge is power, and when someone shares their hopes and dreams with you, they hand you a lot of power. Kathleen Warner, former Executive VP of Economic Development for New York City shares, "In my experience of corporate America, personal information wasn't valued or exalted but used as a sledgehammer or other object of destruction or discrimination."[3]

I am confident that if you are reading this book, this is not the kind of boss you want to be. How you wield power will be your legacy: best boss ever, worst boss ever, or somewhere in between. If you aren't being respectful of the people who work for you, something is wrong, including the possibility that this management curve is the wrong curve for you.

What Is Your Vision for Your New Hire?

Some managers seem to believe that a new hire or reassignment requires nothing from them: this new person can be launched into the fray and expected to mysteriously succeed. With these managers, expectations are unrealistic, decision making is capricious, and metrics arbitrary. Michael Hone, VP of Payor Contracting's select medical division, relates an experience from his career:

> I felt confident when I started . . . I knew I had the skill sets to be successful, though I knew being in a

new company and building a new department while
implementing new reports and processes would be
a challenge. The hard part was that I had only one
month to transition, and I reported to two different
VPs: one in finance (technically my boss) and a VP
of supply chain and logistics. Unexpected tension was
created because each boss had different expectations
on priorities and timelines and silently deferred to me
on how to manage each relationship. Things couldn't
happen fast enough for the supply chain VP. He qui-
etly became upset at my progress, and out of nowhere
decided to put me on a sixty-day notice to improve or
be fired (this was after six months with the company).
I had never been on the wrong side of performance,
ever! As being fired was not an option for me, I discussed a plan with the finance VP (who wanted me
to succeed), for turning things around. I worked long
hours and started to deliver. Meanwhile the supply
chain VP started to take some ownership over what
we would build, including timelines and a resource
plan. I learned a few years later that my experience
with the supply chain VP wasn't unique: many more
people had been fired or left the company in frustration [because of his management style].

If we operate on the assumption that none of us acts
out of malicious intent, maybe the supply chain VP didn't
know what he wanted Michael to do. This happens, not
infrequently. Perhaps we are clear on the functional job but

haven't thought about the psychological role. Or maybe we believe that the person will somehow divine what we want them to do without being told what we want. When we assume that, we'll likely be wrong.

None of us is as comprehensible or knowable as we like to think we are. In her book *No One Understands You and What to Do About It*, Heidi Grant of Columbia Business School and the Neuroleadership Institute helps us understand this phenomenon. Grant became intrigued by this topic when her then-husband, a successful executive, came home perplexed: Why did his employees, colleagues, and others so often mistake his intent? The short answer is, because we all assume our intentions are clear, even when they're not. One of the examples Grant highlights is the work of Jacquie Vorauer and Stephanie-Danielle Claude of the University of Manitoba, in Canada. The researchers examined how readily negotiators detected the goals and intentions of their negotiating partners. The study participants estimated that they had communicated well enough to be understood 60 percent of the time. Their partners reported understanding them only 26 percent of the time.[4]

Every time you speak to your new hire assume that you're not easily being understood and that you're not necessarily understanding what is being communicated to you. There are times when uncertainty is something to be embraced, but this is not one of them. Communicate your expectations clearly. Answer the questions: What do you hope they will accomplish in this role? How do you see them contributing to the team and to the bottom line over time? What do they need to do to be prepared for a next role? What do you need them to do now?

You also want to answer the oft-wondered, but rarely asked question, *How do I manage up?* I confess that I get squeamish when I hear "manage up." I can't help but think of the seemingly spineless J. Pierrepont Finch who rises from window washer to president of Worldwide Wicket Company in *How to Succeed in Business Without Really Trying.* He does it by lying: he tells the head of HR that the CEO has given him a job when he hasn't. He does it by scheming: Finch supports a rival for a promotion—not to be selfless, but because it's a dead-end job. He does it by manipulating: when J. Pierrepont is about to get fired for a snafu, he refers to all his fellow employees as family, saving his skin. Those who equate managing up with being sneaky or downright conniving—doing whatever it takes to climb the career ladder—probably aren't going to be very good at managing up.

Managing up means thinking like a manager even when you aren't. It's about proving, through consistent, proficient work, that you can manage yourself and are therefore capable of increased responsibility.

As your employees share their goals with you, lay out the expectation that they learn to solve problems as they would in the role they aspire to. That's what Mike Kopelman, the junior employee I talked about earlier, who is now Senior VP of finance at HBO, does. "I always take the approach that my primary job is to make my boss be successful," he says. "It's not that I'm not ambitious. But I trust that if I do a good job, my boss will take care of me. Of course, that's more effective when you have a boss who is looking out for your career." Some people come into the workplace intuitively understanding this. Others don't—and it's not something they will learn in school.

For all your junior employees who didn't learn how to manage up in school, be explicit: *I am here to help you help me get my job done. Here's how. I will then reward you for your contributions. And here's how I'll do that.*

As the chess master for your team, are you looking at your new hire as an expendable pawn to be sacrificed for short-term strategy gains? Or as a pawn that can become a queen? As you bring someone new onto the team, what kind of development do you want to occur as they move across the board? You may not know exactly how to help them develop because you are focused on discovery, but you can have a substantive vision. Relay this clearly and your new employee will be poised for a strong start up the S curve. (See the sidebar "The New Hire: The First Six Months.")

Managing the First Six Months

Now that you have the until-you-are-ready-to-jump-to-a-new-curve plan in place, it's time to focus on the first six months of this role and to provide metrics of success. Because the math at the low end of the S curve will have them working hard with seemingly little result, you want to focus on measuring effort and momentum, not just accomplishment.

The New Hire: The First Week

The first week on the job can be daunting for both of you. Joint planning and good communication in the earliest days of their tenure will often determine whether it's possible to build a bridge successfully to your objectives or if you'll burn the resources from which the bridge should be built without ever putting a first beam in place. Here's what I recommend.

1. Explain your vision, or why, for the organization and your team.

2. Ask, What are you trying to accomplish personally in this role? What do you need from me to be successful?

3. Lay out your expectations, rules, and hopes for their contribution.

I had a coaching client who came to me as he was starting a new job in the construction industry. He was optimistic about his plan, as was his employer. That is until he was thrown into combat with no backup and no short-term milestones by which progress could be reckoned. The boss seemed to believe his new hire would be the magic bullet and change everything. When two months had passed—and he wasn't and hadn't—his boss broke the dreaded news: things weren't working. After only a year on the job, he was let go.

The New Hire: The First Six Months

There's much to be done in the months after your new hire comes on board to ensure their success and comfort on your team. Here are some guidelines to follow.

1. Set short-term goals: clearly define one or two projects for your new employee, with maximum budgets and precise deadlines.

2. Build out their internal network. For example, talk to Vikram in marketing and Jasmin in finance during week one. Give your hire credit for having these conversations.

3. Make two lists: "people to help" and "people to look to for guidance."

For new hires, it is vital to set short-term goals. This de facto constraint gives your new employees something to bump up against to assess how well they are doing. Like a skateboarder who gets quick and useful feedback about their various tricks (in the form of falling on asphalt), they'll know that doing X leads to success; not doing X means they'll crash and burn. Tighten the constraint. Increase the pace of the feedback, and employees will learn faster.

Start with a checklist. Measure progress against the plan. For example, sketch out one or two clearly defined projects with precise deadlines and maximum budgets. Make them projects within projects, if necessary, to allow for rapid iteration and quick wins. This will keep them focused on learning and improving rather than being fearful of blowing it.

One of these projects should be building out their network. Provide a list of specific people to reach out to in the first week, then in the second week. Give them credit for having these conversations. Whom do you want them to look to for guidance? Whom do you want them to help? These networking tasks are especially important because they are concrete and easily achievable and because they weave your new hires into the fabric of your organization. The more people they know, the greater their ability to make things happen.

When you provide constraints in the form of clearly scoped projects, they (and you) can receive feedback that will help take account of their progress. Room-escape games are increasingly popular as a corporate team-building activity for that very reason. Locked in a room together, a group of people look for clues and solve puzzles to gain the key to escape. Such exercises expose strengths and weaknesses as individuals cope with constraints. Who communicates well or is calm under pressure? How is a deadline handled? Who are the analytical thinkers, and which team members are more imaginative? Cooperative? Confident? Under normal circumstances we leave a room by opening a door; thinking outside that box is unnecessary. Lock the door and withhold—in other words, embrace constraint—and concealed strengths may be revealed, along with a newfound appreciation for the strengths of their colleagues.

Listen to the New Hire's "Outsider" Ideas

One important milestone during the first six months is to get your new hire's perspective on your operation. It seems like an obvious thing to do, but getting information from someone less experienced can be annoying. They have all these ideas and they question everything: why you do what you do and why you do it the way you do it. So we fight it off.

I recently worked with a CEO whose sales team was at the top of the S curve. To invigorate the team, he hired someone new, at the low end of the curve. It completely backfired. The entrenched employees ran the new hire out, *Hunger Games*–style. This sort of workplace warfare has been termed "gentle mobbing."[5]

When someone new is introduced to your team, how will you as a leader manage the confrontations that may erupt? Aicha Evans, chief strategy officer at Intel and one of the most senior women in the chip industry, has said that when a report comes in and wants to "gently mob" someone, she asks, "Are you escalating this? If you are, then I need to know and we'll get human resources in here." And the mobbing stops.

We all love our comfortable ideas. We cling to the moorings of our established opinions as if for survival. But being able to hear the contrary ideas of others without affront allows us to move more quickly up the learning curve. We may even find ourselves agreeable to things we initially found disagreeable—if we dare to step back and give them a chance. Learn to solicit ideas and opinions from newcomers who aren't yet blind through familiarity. Future performance and innovation may hinge on it.

Jayne Juvan, chair of the private equity legal practice at Tucker Ellis, found that the questioning spirit of a new hire can provide advantages she'd never considered. Midway through a difficult high-risk twin pregnancy, Juvan decided she needed to hire a junior attorney to take on some of her more mundane tasks. Her firm hired Ashley Gault, an attorney who had recently moved back to the area and was just returning to work herself after having her first child. Normally innovative and high-energy, Juvan was exhausted and struggling to keep her head above water with a recent increase in client activity. "Ashley came in like a tornado," Juvan remembers, "eager to rejoin a law firm and enthusiastic about shaking up past practices to plow a better path. When I asked her to print and review contracts for a corporate transaction, she instead sought out resources from our library that would allow her to review the contracts electronically in a more efficient manner, expediting the process and saving client resources. When I said networking was off the table because I could hardly walk, she challenged me and suggested that we line up conference calls. Ashley Gault knew that maintaining a positive mental attitude and continuing to innovate despite real hardships were both key to building and growing a successful legal practice. Because it became a genuine team effort, my practice never declined."

Juvan was hoping a new hire would lighten her load during a vulnerable time, both professionally and personally.

It would have been easy for her to resent Gault and resist her new-fangled ideas. Instead, her willingness to embrace Gault's energy, ideas, and pushback against established norms proved to be an incredible asset to Juvan.

We all marvel at the hugely successful mega-businesses that began in a basement, garage, or shed. They often share a familiar and seemingly unlikely path to success: Someone starts tinkering with an idea. Instead of doing the conventional thing, they are highly unconventional. Your new reports are not likely to be consigned to the company barn to do their work, but tinkering in a garage with an unconventional idea is a low-end-of-the-curve activity, and it can yield striking results. When you aren't yet entrenched in company culture and conventions, when you don't know how to do what you're trying to do, when you haven't yet mastered your responsibilities through the performance of specific, repetitive tasks—this is when eyes and minds are most open to doing something new. Use it to your advantage.

The Six-Month Check-In

If your new hire is still struggling six months into the job, you may be questioning your hiring decision. As we've said, progress will be slow at the low end of the curve. But one can't help wonder: Is it still the low, flat end of an S curve of growth, or is it just a flat line? No one wants to declare a curve dead unless it is, in fact, dead. But if your new hire is on life support, a nudge to a new curve may be unavoidable.

How can you know when it's time to give up or time to have more patience? I have evaluated thousands of new ventures and career-dreamers. Here's what I've learned: if you can answer "yes" to the following questions, your new hire is at the low end of the curve and growth *is* coming.

1. Is this person occupying an otherwise unoccupied niche? When I first moved to equity research, I was hired to cover the cement and construction sector in Latin America. Soon thereafter, our bank merged with another, and they already had a highly ranked cement and construction analyst. When there is an overlap with another employee, there isn't the space to do the job or even a distinctive job to do—and even a true high potential might not have room to grow. Fortunately, there were a number of media companies going public with no analyst to cover them. In assuming coverage of this sector, I moved into an unoccupied niche, and was able to move up the learning curve quickly.

If you've created a new role, it may not be immediately obvious what a new hire will accomplish. You expect they will eventually contribute, and brilliantly, but there aren't yet quantifiable results. They are in good company: many game-changers have garnered little attention in their nascent stages. The Wright brothers tested their flying machines without an audience for years.[6] The first powered flights weren't covered by the press. There was apathy and skepticism. Few outside the immediate neighborhood even believed they'd occurred. The Wrights *were* visionaries; they persevered until their genius flew up the S curve and off the charts. A slow start isn't the whole story.

2. Is this person playing to their strengths? One of the key accelerants of personal disruption is playing to your strengths. Work with employees to identify their unique strengths and then learn to deploy that talent where it will be most effective.

Jocelyn Wong studied engineering at Purdue University before going to work in manufacturing at Procter & Gamble. This is what her father wanted for her, and Jocelyn wanted to make him proud. But she felt trapped. And she wasn't good at her job. Instead of giving up on Jocelyn, berating her, or firing her, her boss asked if there was any other role she'd like to explore. She was, after all, a hard worker. As it turned out, Jocelyn was very good at marketing. Since that fateful day in 2001, she has gone on to become the chief marketing officer at Family Dollar (now Dollar General), and she is currently the CMO at Lowe's, a *Fortune* 40 company. What a waste if P&G had thrown up its hands and given up on her instead of finding a different curve for her to scale.[7]

3. Is the work difficult but not debilitating? For the curve to be difficult is one thing; if it's debilitating, that is something else. An ever-growing body of psychological research indicates that persistence in the face of an unattainable goal adversely affects your quality of life. Concordia University psychologist Carsten Wrosch says, "The disappointment of perpetual failure or shortfall leads to negative effects on biological processes in the endocrine, immune, metabolic, and central nervous systems" with consequences for the development of long-term disease.[8]

Dreading work, or suffering adverse physical conditions or serious emotional ones, are symptoms of a flatlining curve. Learning to disengage from a goal, to stop tilting at unreachable windmills, is an important life and career skill, a self-protective ability that can save your health. It's something we need to help employees do when we realize that they are on the wrong curve.

If, by contrast, people are energized, getting their work done on time and well, consistently coming up with ideas, rest assured that growth is on the way.

4. Is your low-ender gaining momentum? Using the metrics that are appropriate to the situation is key, and at the low end of the S curve, momentum is what you want to measure, not absolute performance. If, for example, last week, your new hire needed eight hours to complete a task that would take an experienced employee one hour, this week, does it take six, or even four hours? The math around exponential growth tells us that the starting point is to a large degree irrelevant. What matters is: Are you growing, and how fast?

One way to track momentum is by pairing your low-ender with other stakeholders—a buddy system—to create goals for what needs to happen over the first few months on this curve. As your new hire becomes publicly accountable for what they need to accomplish, receives feedback from their "buddy," and improves (or not), it will be more and more clear whether this employee is flat-lining or on an upward trajectory.

If you answered "no" to three or more of the questions I've just covered regarding your new hire, it might be time to pull the plug. Any jump to a new curve results in at least a short-term loss of efficiency. And there are plenty of times when the only thing standing between us and the outcome we desire is tenacity. But at other times there's just no viable prescription for success. Believing that additional stretches of time or investment of money will save the day is tempting (we are all sensitive to the sunk-cost fallacy). But knowing when to pull the plug can be the difference between sinking a rowboat and sinking the *Titanic*.

What do you do if a new hire is on the wrong curve? Not only will you know it, but secretly, they probably will know it too, even if they aren't ready to admit it. If you respect their work, you may be able to help them find the right fit within your company, as the senior executive did with Jocelyn Wong. Or they might need to move on. Treat your ex-employees with respect, and they will become lifelong ambassadors for your organization.

Even if a curve has flatlined, experience is a great instructor. Failed adventures help us chart a smarter path the next time. The Sports Performance Research Institute of New Zealand has studied competitive surfers and determined that they typically spend 8 percent of their time riding waves, 54 percent of time paddling, and 28 percent waiting.[9] No one would suggest that the paddling, waiting, and inevitable wipeouts aren't integral to their ultimate success. Like a surfer, the next wave to roll in may well be the S curve you've been waiting for.

Be a CEO (Chief Encouragement Officer)

Devn J. Cornish, a pediatric physician, relates that when he was a young resident at Johns Hopkins, he often felt ill prepared and unintelligent when he compared himself to other interns. He shares that in his third month, he was sitting in the nurse's station late one night, "alternately sobbing to myself and falling asleep as I tried to write the admission orders for a small boy with pneumonia. I had never felt so discouraged in my life. I didn't have any idea how to treat pneumonia in a ten-year-old." At that moment, one of the senior residents put his hand on Cornish's shoulder and asked how he was doing. After pouring out his frustrations, the resident "told me how proud he and all of the other senior residents were of me and how they felt like I was going to be an excellent doctor. He believed in me at a time when I didn't even believe in myself."[10]

One of the biggest challenges of being on the low end of the curve is that people work hard, but they feel like their work isn't very good (and they may be right). Feeling the agitation or disapproval of you, their boss, increases the weight of concern. Remember they took this job and will stay in this job—or not—largely because of you. If you can make them feel safe in exploring this new S curve and acknowledge their efforts (even when their performance is less than perfect), you're sitting on a gold (and copper) mine.

Summary

- The low end of the curve is home to new hires and early-career professionals, as well as experienced and late-career professionals. Regardless, manage all as newcomers to their learning curve. You optimize your team with 15 percent of your people.

- Low-end challenges are made more manageable when we can convey to the new hire our vision for the organization and for them within that paradigm.

- Invest in frequent, honest communication about what you need and expect from your low-ender, and encourage them to be equally open about what they need from you to develop in their role.

- Some of the accelerants of personal disruption are particularly relevant at the outset of a new role. Ensure these are understood and used to best advantage.

- Consistent evaluation of the low-ender's momentum, as well as their fit with the rest of the team, helps address problems in a timely manner and allow for adjustment. It also gives early warning if the curve or team fit is not working well, alerting to dysfunction within the team.

5

PLAYING TO THEIR STRENGTHS

Give people slightly more trust, freedom, and authority
than you are comfortable giving them. If you're not
nervous, you haven't given them enough.

—**Lazlo Bock**

Telisa Yancy is the chief marketing officer at American Family
Insurance (AFI). It's her dream job. Before arriving at
AFI seven years ago, she filled substantial roles with iconic
American brands such as Burger King and Ford. She's
worked hard to move up the ranks. One might excuse
her for relaxing a bit. But her boss has a different agenda.
AFI's CEO, Jack Salzwedel, doesn't want her to be a mid-
dling CMO, he wants her to be exceptional. Yancy credits
Salzwedel for always pushing her and never allowing her to
be complacent or mediocre in her role. He doesn't hesitate
to dole out stretch assignments—and send people back to
the drawing board, more than once, to improve and refine

their efforts. "He's not afraid to put you in a crucible to help the company and you personally," says Yancy. "He always challenges me to be more, give more, serve more, do more, dream more."[1]

This is what the most engaging part of the learning curve feels like: that "sweet spot" when you're no longer a confused beginner but aren't yet a slightly bored master. A good boss understands how to lengthen this most productive stretch of the curve, where a person has achieved competency but hasn't yet been overtaken by stagnation. There is energy and power here. Ideally, 70 percent of your team will be in this sweet spot.

At the low end of the learning curve, your new hires experienced the natural constraints of inexperience. You imposed constraints in the form of milestone checkpoints to provide quick feedback and gauge momentum and helped them recalibrate when necessary. Now it's time to reevaluate: Does an artificial constraint need to be imposed—a new stretch goal, for example? On the steep part of the curve is where people perform proactively. Where they think creatively. Where they innovate. It is a sweet spot indeed, and many of your people are there right now—your job is to maximize what they are already primed to do.

Stretch Assignments and the Law of Friction

In physics, there is the law of friction. "We think of it as bad," says physics teacher Tina John, granddaughter of famed physicist Harvey Fletcher. "It makes motors and shoes wear out. We could all slide along faster if friction didn't slow us down. But if there is no friction, you can't even start moving." For a person to move forward from standing still requires pushing against the ground. The ground then propels us forward. This is Newton's third law: for every action, there is an equal and opposite reaction. Think about an icy hill in the winter. Your car spins its wheels because there is nothing to push off against. Because of gravity, we need friction to change direction, go around a corner—and to move up a curve.

Apply this to the sweet-spot dwellers on your team. They may seem to be doing just fine, sliding along with zero friction. Passing their workdays in a pleasant glide. But we don't slide uphill to great achievement or coast our way to the top of an S curve.

Friction was intrinsic at the beginning, at the low end of the curve. As low-enders gain traction, natural friction dissipates, leading to loss of momentum. You can reintroduce friction by giving your employees a business challenge that's not quite within their grasp, a force to push against that requires greater investment of effort to maintain momentum or even to accelerate it.

This can come in the form of stretch assignments. When challenged, 67 percent of people will demonstrate above-average creativity. Only 33 percent of people show above-average creativity in nonchallenging roles.[2] Ideally, you'll finesse assignments to fit within the Goldilocks rule: too big and you're back to the low end of the curve, with work that can be so difficult that it can be crippling. Too small and it isn't going to require stretching. You want to be in the land of "just right."

There's an orderly relationship between a task's complexity and our enjoyment of it. It's an inverted U-function when mapped on a graph. If the x-axis plots how difficult a task is and the y-axis plots how much we like it, if you're at the bottom left of the graph, the task is too easy and therefore not much fun. As the task gets harder, the enjoyment level will rise as well. Challenge and fun remain positively correlated for quite a while, until a personal threshold is crossed. Eventually something becomes too formidable, enjoyment decreases, and you hate what you are doing. The Yerkes-Dodson law says that when stress is either too low or too high, performance declines.[3]

Lisa Joy Rosner, former CMO of Neustar, shares an experience from her university years, when she opted to take a certain course despite the fact that the professor, Jackson Bryer, had a reputation as being the most exacting teacher in the English literature department. She enjoyed the reading, class discussion was lively, and when her first paper was due, she worked hard and turned in what she was sure was a top-notch product. Imagine her dismay when it was returned to her heavily marked up and graded with a C-plus.

Eventually she went to discuss the grade with Bryer. When she appeared at his door, he told her he'd been expecting her. "If any other student had turned in that paper, they would have gotten an A. I hold you to a higher standard. I do not want ordinary 'A' work out of you. I want exceptional 'A-plus' work out of you, and I am going to teach you how to do it."

He became a genuine mentor, and the will to excel that he instilled has influenced Rosner throughout her life and career. Timid management can be a career breaker. Great management can be a career maker.

Sweet-spot employees are confident in their abilities, having moved past the daily struggle at the low end of the curve. Yet it is common for managers to be reluctant to provide these employees with stretch assignments. That may be because these workers are high potentials, and you don't want to discourage or derail them. But experiencing a genuine risk of failure is what motivates most of us to step up to the plate. Consider the tendency of top-ranking athletic teams to have some of their worst performances against poor-quality opponents. Allow, and even generate, opposition. It's the friction that propels us onward and upward.[4]

A new stretch assignment doesn't mean hands-off; in fact, you may want to be even more involved, actively coaching your employee. Naveen Rajdev, chief marketing officer of tech giant Wipro, shared with me a life-altering encounter with his best boss, a mentor who gifted Rajdev with a lesson that transformed his management style. Rajdev had a large deal in the works with a potential client. Because it was highly competitive, he was seeking leeway to offer a discount. His boss gave him the green light but warned him that discounting might cause Rajdev to fall short of profitability targets and trigger a domino effect on thousands of employees. "They may not get their quarterly bonus," Rajdev was reminded, which they might be counting on to buy a car, for a house down payment, to help with education expenses, or to accomplish some other significant personal or family objective. In the end, Rajdev won the deal without offering the client a discount. "I think everyone became more human to me," Rajdev reflects. He thinks about people's needs more now, for every decision he makes. "I see a bubble of dreams, like a cartoon, above everyone's head. And I have no right to pop it."

But the challenge we give our employees must be achievable. We are trying to create circumstances in which failure, while a genuinely possible outcome, isn't a predetermined one. Consider the successful professional who was hired to increase sales for a small but well-established language translation firm that targeted clients in the medical and pharmaceutical industries. The owner of the company wanted to grow revenue by 200 percent over five years. But the salesperson hired to make that goal a reality soon discovered that there was no intent to hire additional project managers or other staff to handle the new business. There was no plan to upgrade to state-of-the-art technologies. The business had been built on quick-turnaround translation projects of a few hard-copy pages each (most translation work today is done digitally, with little volume in hard copy work). After a few months of intense discussions, it became clear that the owner wanted to triple revenue selling translation services a page or two at a time, like they'd always done. The sales professional jumped to a more promising curve. Unrealistic objectives and expectations drive disengagement.

Most people, including those playing on your team, want to bring their intellectual prowess, creative gifts, and their time and effort to the table to address important issues. Make sure your employees understand what you envision for the company, team—and especially for them. Then give them a big problem to solve.

Stretch Assignments Aren't Your Only Tool

Even without a new stretch assignment where you are adding something, you can keep your high-performing employee engaged by taking something away—by imposing the right constraints. That may sound counterintuitive, given that these are your most competent employees, the ones you can rely on to perform their jobs well. Why would you want to restrict them in any way?

When I work with organizations, we do an exploratory exercise that helps leaders reframe their constraints as a positive. In the case of your sweet-spot employees, consider imposing constraints that fall into the following categories:

Time

For almost everyone, time is the biggest constraint. A task that is less demanding becomes a major challenge if you impose a tight deadline. In many situations, time constraints are already built in. If they are not, here are some questions to ask your employees, and yourself.

- To hit annual targets in nine months instead of twelve, what would you do differently?

- If you were going to be away for three months, what would you do to make sure things could run without you? (The answer can provide solutions as you deal with health issues, pregnancies and new babies, aging, and so on.)

- What are the most important priorities? Which things aren't as important? What must you absolutely get done so that your manager can advocate for your jump to a new curve?

- What doesn't require human resources to accomplish? A university professor friend was drowning in a sea of tests to grade. A colleague suggested he hire a teaching assistant to help. Instead, he found a way to automate with an app that can grade multiple-choice question tests in a matter of minutes, rather than hours.

- If you knew that your star performers would be in their current assignment for no more than three years, what would you do differently?

Money

"If only I had enough money." We've all heard that. We've all said that. As with time, we think constrictively when funds are limited. I frequently hear aspiring entrepreneurs say, "If I could raise money, then I could start a business." A postmortem performed on two hundred failed startups found that the number-one reason the funded startups failed was that they ran out of cash; for unfunded startups, this was only reason number ten.[5] Adequate funding is not a panacea, and empty pockets don't necessarily doom us. If you have an idea, a simple question to ask is, "What is the simplest, cheapest way to test that idea?" Here are some other specific questions you can use to challenge the team.

- If your business unit had to be profitable as a stand-alone entity, what would your business model be?

- If you had to increase your margins to next year's target *this* year, what would you do?

- If you only had half of the current marketing budget, what would you do differently?

- If you had to manufacture a product with 25 percent fewer components, what would you do?

- If you had to cut your budget in half and still deliver the same product or service, what would you do?

- If you had to assemble an A-team with only 80% of your current budget, what would you do?

After discussing these questions, ask your employees, "Why wouldn't you do this now?"

"Necessity is the mother of invention." This handy aphorism encapsulates the reality that desperation and disruption—and its innovative impulse—often go hand in hand. When there is no ladder, we try a rope. When we are at the end of our rope, we throw a belt over a zip-line and slide down it like James Bond. Right? When we are out of money, when we've exhausted the possibilities available through conventional channels, we explore or invent a new channel.

Expertise

The world needs experts, but it also needs novices. Sometimes the best ideas emerge from not knowing the conventions or "how it's done." To see how a lack of expertise can become a valuable constraint, ask yourself and your employee:

- What problems would your competitors who know little about the business (low-end disruptors and the 15 percent of your people at the low end of the curve) be "dumb" enough to think they can solve?

- If you were CEO for a day and ran the company based on your area of expertise, what would you change?

- What if everyone on your team were new? No experts, only novices. What would you do differently?

Buy-In

The challenge to expertise constraints is getting buy-in. When an expert has an idea, people are much more likely to green-light it. So one of the most important things you can do is require expertise-constrained team members to learn to solicit and get approval for their initiatives. Even when you know it makes sense to say "yes," require your workers to make their case in a way that would earn buy-in.

To help them with this, you might ask:

- If you had to get buy-in for your idea from a ten-year-old, what would you say?

- If you had to explain your idea to a person who speaks a different language, how would you modify your approach?

- Suppose you are in marketing. How would you persuade the finance team to give your idea the go-ahead? For the product team, how would you adjust your approach?

- When you are ready to jump to a new S curve, how will you make the case that your move will be beneficial not only to you, but to the boss you are leaving behind?

Whenever you propose a new idea, you are asking your colleagues and boss to jump to a new S curve. Which is scary for them. Remember we tend to like the safety of our own ideas. So how can you explain your initiative in a way that makes it less risky for others, for your boss, and your boss's boss?

Give People Real Responsibility

An excellent fictional example of utilizing constraints to drive people up the learning curve is Orson Scott Card's book *Ender's Game*, a masterpiece of military science fiction. Ender, while still a young boy, has been sent to a

Constraints to Keep Sweet-Spot Employees Disrupting

When you see that your employee needs to be challenged to stay engaged, it's time to consider some specific parameters of constraint. Here are some categories to consider when you're ready to put on the pressure.

1. TIME: Add a "brick wall" deadline for greater challenge, move annual targets up, automate, and prioritize.

2. MONEY OR OTHER RESOURCES: Impose resource limitations to stretch workers' creativity. Ask what they would do differently with half the budget, fewer marketing dollars, the need to bring a new product to market faster, or the need to assemble an A-team on a budget.

3. EXPERTISE: Challenge your employee to approach problems as a novice.

4. BUY-IN: Ask that your sweet-spot employees learn to sell their innovative ideas to others on your team and up the office hierarchy as if they were customers, because they are.

battle school to save the world. By playing war games in a way that no one else has thought of playing them, he becomes the most successful general in the school's history. He also has huge constraints. He gets unwanted soldiers, the ones everyone else rejects. Nor does he have enough soldiers, time, or adult supervision. Yet his commanding officer, Colonel Graff, says this lack of resources is crucial. "Ender must believe that no matter what, no adult will ever, ever step in to help in any way. If he does not believe that to the core of his soul, he will never reach the peak of his ability." If the people who work for you don't get real responsibility—the kind of assignments that could lead to a large-scale failure but also to engagement, innovation, and higher profitability—they will never reach the peak of their ability.

Vala Afshar, now chief evangelist at Salesforce.com, was trained as an engineer. Earlier in his career, he worked as VP of software quality and VP of services at Enterasys, a company that produced networking hardware and software. When Chris Crowell was hired as CTO and became Afshar's boss, one of Crowell's first moves was to eliminate some of Afshar's engineering responsibilities. Crowell believed that the "one thing [customers] cherish more than anything is customer support, over features and functions, even pricing," so he told Afshar to focus solely on customer service and support. Crowell told Afshar: "I am doing this because it is the most important thing for your career and your company."

Over the next few years, Crowell gave Afshar several stretch assignments, eventually promoting him to chief customer officer, through which he was responsible for seven call centers, a hundred call center professionals, educational services, and a $200 million-plus business unit. When Crowell eventually became the CEO, and after wrestling through several CMOs, he tapped Afshar to become CMO of the $400 million company. On the face of it, this wasn't an obvious move. But, Crowell shares, "Vala had great ideas, the best material in terms of presenting our products. He had a strong following among team members. And he was customer-focused because he was customer facing. It wasn't that hard of a jump to promote him."

Were it not for Crowell pushing him in a different direction, says Afshar, "I would [still] be in a lab with engineering, building and testing and releasing products." Crowell's willingness to push Afshar in a new direction and give him a responsibility—with the risk of a material failure—gave him the opportunity to see what he was capable of.

Think of spring bulbs, like daffodils and hyacinths. They need to go through a period of cold weather to flourish. Gardeners either plant them in the ground in the fall and let nature do its work, or they pot up the bulbs and chill them somewhere cool for two months before bringing them into a warmer area to signal to the bulb that it's time to bud. The bulb doesn't know or care whether the cold is real or artificial; what matters is that without that temperature constraint, it would never burst into flower. Shortfalls of time, money, expertise, and buy-in lend themselves to a strategy that favors disruption. Your job is to provide the soil, to impose the constraints, that allow your employees to bloom.

Support Them and Keep Them Happy

I realize I've talked a lot in this chapter about constraints and failure. This might sound like tough medicine. And yet, most us know from experience that management is most effective when constraints and the possibility of a bona fide failure are paired with meaningful support.

Ilana Golan was an F-16 flight instructor in the Israeli Air Force and a commander with oversight of all F-16 pilots. She and her team completely overhauled the training and education program for pilots, a feat for which she received a best commander award.

At twenty-three, she became an engineering student and an intern at Intel in Haifa, Israel. In a sense, she was at the bottom of the curve—a student intern—despite the weighty responsibilities she had shouldered in the military. Together, Golan and her boss, Ziyad Hanna, Senior Principal Engineer and Formal Verification Leader, analyzed which big engineering problems would need to be solved in the future. They knew their verification tools were inadequate for the next generation of chips due to their logical complexities; the current software would either run out of time or out of memory.

Hanna put Golan in charge of finding a solution. She started with academia, but it was too theoretical. She then surveyed startups, but this was 1997, and pickings were relatively slim. However, with Hanna's help, she identified a startup in Sweden, Prover Technology, that was working on software solutions for increasing capacity and reliability for railway infrastructure. Intel invited the Prover management team to Haifa.

Jointly, they spent a week analyzing the railway-related software. Believing the algorithms and heuristics used by Prover Technology could apply to chips, Hanna then sent Golan to Sweden to work with Prover and to build a prototype. They conducted a thorough benchmark test to see how well the prototype functioned and to determine whether they should build or buy (create equivalent software in-house or shorten the timeline by buying the Swedish software). Intel eventually purchased the software for a few million dollars. It was used for decades and was the kernel of Jasper Design Automation, a formal verification company for systems on a chip, that was later sold to Cadence Design Systems for $150 million.

In giving Golan this stretch assignment, Hanna took a risk. He mitigated the risk by mentoring her. "Ziyad is very technical," Ilana says, "so I needed to talk in technical terms. I had to explain clearly why it would work. He had a great balance between letting me feel freedom and trusting me to roll up my sleeves and helping me in a hands-on way."

Hanna, now VP of R&D at Cadence, understood how to get the most out of a sweet-spot employee: he gave Golan a stretch assignment, with plenty of support and collaboration and the highest expectations for her ultimate success. Says Golan, "I didn't realize what a remarkable boss he was until I became a boss."

It's easy to ignore the employees on this, the steep part of the learning curve. These are your happiest, most engaged, most productive people. They can be quite a contrast to the low- or high-end employees, where you need to be more hands-on, either because they are struggling or you are panicking because they are going to leave.

But sweet-spot employees need management too. Keep them happy! Pay is a shorthand way of signaling value, on both an absolute and a relative basis. If you've been in the workforce long enough, you may have experienced a situation where the performance metrics indicated you outperformed your peers, but you were paid the same amount or even less. Perhaps your contribution was something not easily measured, such as soft skills, or your ability to enable an employee to jump to a new curve, which created value for the team or company at a cost to you or your group. The truth is that there are few things harder to stomach in the workplace than being underpaid. Financial compensation is your starting and ending point. Get that right, and you signal to your employees that you are worthy of their trust.

You can add to your financial show of good faith with intangibles, like providing ongoing training. In my coaching at Harvard Business School executive education, I have been surprised that frequently the C-suite executives were tapped to attend not because their company wanted to train them but because the firm was afraid they would leave. You lessen the risk of losing high-performing people by making the investment when they want it, not when you need it.

You also show your star performers they are valued by giving them the spotlight. Consider Gina Moshier, director of organizational effectiveness at AgChoice Farm Credit in

Mechanicsburg, Pennsylvania. AgChoice is one of nineteen entities within the larger AgFirst Farm Credit system. Her boss, CEO Darrell Curtis, hired her right out of school in 2004. She holds a bachelor's of science degree in animal sciences, a master's of science degree in organizational development, and started as a credit analyst. Moshier has repeatedly been given new curves to jump to, and she's continually added value to the company. She's in the sweet spot of her current curve, overseeing training and development and IT implementation.

I recently facilitated a working session for AgFirst Farm Credit, which included, among others attendees, Curtis and Moshier. Not only was Curtis willing to showcase Moshier in front of the CEO at AgFirst, he openly praised her and willingly made her available to share her wealth of knowledge with executives across the Farm Credit system. "I'm lucky to work at AgChoice," says Moshier. "Darrell continually supports my personal growth and challenges me to find new ways to make a difference. It's easy to work hard when you have fun doing what you love."

Summary

- To keep your team at its most effective, aim for 70 percent of your people to be in the sweet spot of their learning curve at any given time.

- When natural constraints have dissolved, you may consciously impose constraints of time, money, expertise, and buy-in. These forces can help bring to the fore the resourcefulness that stimulates innovation.

- Increased ease can be accompanied by a loss of momentum. Provide stretch assignments and the real possibility of failure to reintroduce the friction that is a natural feature of beginning on a new learning curve.

- Sweet-spot employees are easy to forget about because everything is working. Remember to show that you value them.

MANAGING MASTERS

There is a moment, a cusp . . . we are never so
wise as when we live in this moment.

—Paul Kalanithi, *When Breath Becomes Air*

George Washington, familiar as a war hero and the first
president of the United States, struggled with an issue many
managers face: allowing a top-performing staff member to
jump to a new learning curve.[1] Alexander Hamilton was
Washington's secretary, his most capable aide, for four years.
Hamilton recognized that wartime provided opportunities to
demonstrate his abilities and further his ambitions. Extraor-
dinarily gifted, he possessed the commensurate desire to
advance in rank. He became insistent, ever more eager as
time passed, but Washington turned him down, claiming
that he couldn't promote Hamilton over full colonels.

The real problem for Washington was that no one could
match Hamilton's writing ability. After being in "hourly

contact with Washington for four years, Hamilton had become [Washington's] alter ego," says biographer Ron Chernow. He "was able to capture [Washington's] tone on paper or in person. Hamilton was a casualty of his own success." When he finally had the courage to disagree with a man for whom most people had "God-like awe," there was a falling-out. Unlike what other bosses might have done, Washington made a "large-hearted, conciliatory gesture": he apologized and "reluctantly honored" Hamilton's decision to leave his staff.

Here's the challenge: after months, maybe years of investment, our employee shoots up the learning curve. They have become our go-to person, willing and able to do whatever is asked. We've become accustomed to an outsized return on this stellar employee. Why would we push them to try something new, when we're still reaping the rewards of our investment? Like Washington, we like our high performers right where they are, where they do us the most good.

But if we are managing for engagement (and innovation), this is the danger zone where boredom, complacency, entitlement, and stagnation do their mischief. As growth peaks and flattens out, if change isn't on the horizon, our high performer may gradually—or not so gradually—become a low performer. They will stop doing their best work because they're no longer challenged to do so. This is seldom intentional, but it happens anyway, either because they feel stymied, their ambition thwarted, or because work has become too easy, and routine is boring. They may even be feeling, like you, comfortable where they are. The urgency and pressure of earlier times has eased, but so has the friction that moved them forward.

When your team member has reached the pinnacle of their learning curve, they may express it openly (as a desire to learn something new or to leave your organization for a challenge elsewhere), or it may become clear through changes in their approach to work (they are less driven, coasting on past success). With a leap to a new curve imminent (more on this in chapter 7), make the most of the time that remains by identifying and exploiting opportunities for them to contribute.

Have Your Best Workers Share What They Know

High-end-of-the-curve employees are skating across a plateau, teetering on a precipice. They are also the most experienced members of your team, and optimally you'll want 15 percent of your people here at any given time. So how can you manage this human resource you've worked hard to develop in a way that will work for your organization, your team, and you?

Start by making use of their mental bandwidth. Task them with sharing their competency. While they're waiting to jump to their next curve, deploy them on crucial, but often neglected, tasks like setting the pace, passing along the tribal memory, and facilitating collaborations between less-experienced employees. Specifically, there are three important roles they can play:

1. Pacesetters: pushing low-enders to excel

2. Trainers: conveying corporate memory

3. Mentors: facilitating collaboration

Pacesetters: Pushing Less-Skilled Employees to Excel

Thelma Schoonmaker has edited films for Martin Scorsese for more than forty years. That's a long time to be at the top of the heap. Perhaps she's stayed at the top because she finds satisfaction in pushing those around her to succeed.

Kyle Ann Stokes, best known for her work on *The Thomas Crown Affair*, was Schoonmaker's protégé. Schoonmaker "was at the top of her game, one of the best, but never acted like a diva," says Stokes. "She was always very human, and lovely, gracious, and kind." She made Stokes feel comfortable asking questions and never considered her to be a bother. Schoonmaker also pushed Stokes: big projects, tight deadlines. When Stokes nailed it, she recalls, "There were fresh flowers (sweet peas) on her workbench. [Schoonmaker was always] a joy to be around."

Schoonmaker could have been a prima donna. Instead, she used her experience to bring colleagues up the learning curve. Put your top performers to good use by showing low-enders what success looks like.

Trainers: Passing On What They Know

David Warsen, a principal electrician for 39 years at the office furniture manufacturer Steelcase, turned 65 in February 2017. Rather than leave the plant cold turkey, he opted into a phased retirement plan. The plan was launched in 2012 to stem the flood of outgoing expertise as baby boomers retired. "It's a win-win because David has vast experience and skills we're short on," says Steve Kempler, manager of skilled trades at the Steelcase plant in Kentwood, Michigan. Warsen reduced his hours from a six-day-a-week full-time schedule to 30 hours a week over four weekdays. "There's a need for more companies to do this if they want to preserve their best practices, innovations, and customer relations," says Paul Irving, chairman of the Milken Institute Center for the Future of Aging. "And there's receptivity among older workers, a majority of whom want to stay engaged and keep working, but in new ways."[2]

Mentors: Encouraging Others to Take New Leaps

Kimberley Krakowski, formerly the informatics manager at Inova Health System in Washington, DC, was looking for candidates for an informatics analyst role when one résumé stood out: that of Carolyn Lopez, who had been a bedside nurse for eighteen years before shifting to clinical documentation. After Lopez had trained sixteen thousand end users during the organization's rollout of an electronic record health initiative, Lopez's role was no longer necessary. Krakowski had by chance observed Lopez in that job and was impressed by her work ethic. She decided to hire Lopez and coach her up the learning curve.

Lopez recalls that Krakowski, though younger than she, was an impactful mentor as they worked together from 2013 until 2017. Krakowski provided unexpected opportunities for Lopez to be a presenter at national conferences and walked her through how to turn her work into a presentation that could be adapted for different audiences.

Under Krakowski's tutelage, Lopez earned additional educational degrees and certifications, and advanced to senior informatics analyst in one year. The next year, when Krakowski moved to a more senior role, Lopez took over for her as informatics manager. Lopez has been honored by Inova as IT Nurse of the Year for nursing excellence in management and as a finalist for the 2017 Leadership Excellence Award. She attributes her great success in this most recent career iteration to Krakowski. "Kimmie constantly challenged me to set higher professional goals and then supported me so I could achieve them," she says.

In many ways, mentoring continues the long tradition of master–apprentice relationships that were once the principal way that knowledge and expertise were transmitted from skilled workers of one generation to the up-and-coming workers in the next. Mentoring of this sort was often the sole source of schooling and job training available for craftspeople and tradespeople in the days before higher education became widespread.

A dynamic mentoring program can help low-end curve-surfers reach competency more quickly and increase the number of workers available to take the place of high-enders as they move on to new curves. But the benefits of mentoring go beyond the advantage it provides for novice employees: It offers a fresh angle on the job for someone who may be a bit idle while they await the jump to a new curve, and it disperses the training responsibility through a wider pool of talent.

Bring Those at the Top Down to Earth

What if despite your best efforts to keep the work interesting, and despite encouraging your top-of-the-curve masters to become mentors, they still seem a little too complacent, a little too comfortable? What do you do about people who have paid their dues, are at the top of the curve, and they like it?

These employees are not to be confused with those who have been in a role for an extended period but are still at peak performance. No, I'm talking about people who not only like things as they are but feel threatened (often without consciously recognizing it) by anything or anyone that could mess with their cozy station. In trying to buffer themselves from change, they become critics of the innovators who threaten them with the change they fear. In such cases, there's an overtone of *That's not how we do it here.*

So how do you deal with these critics? Those who are, often by accident, squelching the very innovation that is the lifeblood of a successful business?

Start with Yourself

Helen Jane Hearn was the director of content strategy at Federated Media, a digital-influencer marketing agency; she was at the top of her S curve. Mary Gail Pezzimenti, former managing editor at *GQ*, was brought in at the same level but then became Helen Jane's boss. This was awkward, but Helen Jane was humble enough to realize she could learn a lot from Mary Gail, not only about print media but also about managing people. Mary Gail had her team take Gallup's popular StrengthsFinder test. "Then she did something none of my bosses had done," Helen Jane says of Mary Gail "She said, 'Helen Jane, you are great at working on fast-paced, quick-turnaround projects. Sue is good at wrapping up long-term programs. This project has both elements. Learn from each other and support each other.'" It's telling that this seemingly obvious management technique was unprecedented in Helen Jane's experience, but terrific that Mary Gail identified her employees' strengths and directed their efforts to be cooperative rather than competitive.

Meanwhile, Mary Gail had a learning curve of her own. She didn't know digital. Fortunately, ego and being the smartest person around weren't priorities for her. Instead of co-opting credit for the expertise that Helen Jane possessed, as managers sometimes do, Mary Gail acknowledged publicly Helen Jane's contribution. Top of the curve, bottom of the curve—wherever you are, you gain moral authority when you are willing to change yourself.

Employ "Righteous Shame"

When everyone is clear about expectations and the rules, you can judiciously leverage a little peer pressure to encourage the reluctant top-ender to change. Venkat Rajendran, a serial entrepreneur whose most recent venture is ConvertCart, an e-commerce platform, was among the early founders of C-DOT, India's telecommunications enterprise, one of the first dozen or so employees in a business that has grown to approximately six hundred. He relates an experience in which his then-boss, Sam Pitroda (remember him from chapter 2), employed righteous shame.

C-DOT had taken two floors of a five-star hotel for their workspace. Upon discovering that the main boardroom had a broken doorknob, they called a handyman. The repair was made and the handyman was about to leave the boardroom—and the mess he'd made fixing the door. He didn't consider cleaning to be part of his job. Pitroda, the head of C-DOT, a powerful man who had a direct line of communication to India's prime minister, thought differently. Pitroda asked for a broom, invited the handyman to sit in a chair, and tidied up while he watched. The message was clear: *You made this mess. You can clean this up. It is not beneath your dignity.* Word of this exchange spread quickly through the organization. Sometimes, a good example is the best way to get the job done.

Moral suasion and righteous shame are a powerful combination. When we willingly disrupt ourselves, we'll hold the upper hand in dealing with the entitlement that can creep up on top-of-the-curve employees.

Don't Sugarcoat It

If someone's performance has gone downhill, it's your job as their boss to tell them—even if it seems like it's not a great time or you're worried that the conversation might go badly. It's not only the respectful thing to do; chances are, if your employee really is a master, they probably already know there's some kind of problem (even if they don't agree with you on what it is).

Josh Coffin holds a customer-facing role at Workday, an enterprise-software firm for financial and human resources. He works with clients to help them scale their business from a financial and human resources perspective and then works with product managers to build those resources. During his first year, he earned great reviews. He then got a new manager, Pete Marcotty, who had a different, more hands-on leadership style. It threw Coffin off. Meanwhile, his wife was pregnant with their third child and experiencing complications. Concerned about his wife, and miffed that "things were being done differently," his performance dipped.

Once his wife had safely given birth and Coffin had returned from paternity leave, Marcotty told him his performance had become subpar. Tough to say. Tough to hear. Importantly though, Marcotty didn't disengage. He encouraged Coffin and gave him a solid new assignment, telling him he needed to make specific changes and reassuring him that once he made those changes he'd be back on track. Six months later, Marcotty was pleased with Coffin's performance and told him so. Pete Marcotty's willingness to be forthright helped Josh Coffin reconcile his differences and swing his performance back to excellence.

Let Them Feel the Risk of Failure

One of the reasons it's hard to get university professors to change is that tenure ensures their job security: they have absolutely nothing to lose by embracing self-satisfied comfort with the status quo. Depending on the discipline, they can get by without updating their lecture notes for decades. I had uninspiring courses with some of these professors, as I suspect most of us did. There is insight in this dialogue from the 1987 film *Moonstruck*: "I teach these classes I've taught for a million years. The spontaneity went out of it for me a long time ago. I started off, I was excited about something, and I wanted to share it. Now it's rote, it's the multiplication table . . . I'm just a burned-out old gasbag." The university professor in question, long disengaged from his work, seeks fulfillment through serial philandering among his female students. This is a movie, of course, fiction not fact, but it is true to the reality that a great deal of career self-sabotage results from boredom settled in at the top of the curve. How would this character's arc have been different if he'd been continuously challenged whenever complacency crept in?

An employee who feels the platform burning under their feet is motivated to jump. This does not require heavy-handed threats, only a challenging new assignment. In such cases, fear of failure can be a useful tool of motivation. We can help people see what failure might look like, that it is real—and that it really can happen to them. We talk a lot about carrots, the incentive dangled attractively to get someone moving. There are times, of course, when this works and is appropriate. But fear of the stick is not to be overlooked.

Of course, when you give your employees daunting assignments, some of them will not succeed. When an employee toward the low end of a learning curve fails, it's not disastrous or even really that surprising: they're brand new at what they're doing, and they are still learning. Training or knowledge may be inadequate. You can help them get more of both.

But when someone toward the top of the learning curve fails, even one of your stars, it's a little more complicated. Often, super-proficient people are stunned to have failed. You, as their manager, may be rather shocked by it as well. The way you react to their failure is going to be instructive, not just for the employee in question but also for the other employees you manage who are watching how you handle it.

Alan Mulally (whom you met in chapter 1) provides a great example of how a leader's reaction to failure can either support innovation or hinder it. Mulally was brought in to turn around an ailing Ford Motor Company.[3] An engineer by training, who before Ford was the CEO of Boeing Commercial Planes, was—and still is—a big proponent of a working-together management system both in terms of process and of expected behaviors. During Ford's weekly executive team business plan review meetings, he would ask for a report on the status of every new automobile product program. The status of these product programs would be color-coded based on their technical, schedule, and financial plan: green for product programs on track or ahead of their plan, yellow for those with potential concerns, and red for those off their plan. For the first six weeks, every single program was coded green. Mulally had promised that honesty wouldn't be penalized, but no one believed him. Under previous regime cultures, leaders were scared to share their problem areas, because the accepted culture dictated that you only surfaced a problem when you had a solution for it.

When a senior executive finally decided to enter the high-stakes ring and display red as the status for the launch of the new Ford Edge, there was dead silence. *Dead man walking,* thought one of his peers. But suddenly, there was applause. It was Mulally, who thanked the senior executive. "That is great visibility. Who can help with this problem?" Mulally identifies this as "the defining moment for the transformation of the Ford culture. Now everyone knew they could trust me and trust the process." Once people knew they wouldn't be fired, or even shamed, they could share their real status against their plan and work together to find solutions to get back on track. This clarity of vision, strategy, openness, transparency, and collaboration became the foundation of a spectacular turnaround, one that eventually led *Chief Executive* magazine to name Mulally CEO of the Year in 2011.[4]

I wanted to understand how Mulally thought about failure. When I spoke with him, he essentially said, "I don't." He is one of the sunniest people you'll ever meet, and his attitude is *I don't think about or see failure.* For me, that answer was astonishing: the fear of failure is one of the reasons why disrupting ourselves tends to be so difficult. Mulally then shared his insights on how he led Ford to such heights, and it's a lesson for a lifetime. "Success is everyone knowing the plan," he said. That means knowing "the status and forecast against the plan, the areas that need special attention to get back on plan, and [being willing to work] together to move from red to yellow to green. There are no failures. Knowing the status, the problems, and the challenges are the gems. With this attitude and transparency, we can work together to deliver toward the plan, the strategy, and the vision." That is how Mulally built an A-team at Ford—and became a leader that people love and want to work for.

If something goes wrong, especially if it goes seriously wrong, what you as the leader do to support your employee will make a huge difference. So make it your mission to fix the problem rather than wasting time and expending effort assigning blame. Like Mulally, in a single stroke you can demonstrate that failure doesn't precipitate a witch hunt. In 1963, philosopher and academic Donald Schön wrote in *Harvard Business Review*, "The new idea either finds a champion or dies."[5] This is also true for people. Every individual who jumps to an S curve is innovating. They have become a stranger in a strange new S-curve land. Without a champion, they wither and die. Do you champion your people? Are the people who work for you afraid to fail or to even make a mistake? These are good questions for all of us to ask. And it leads to many more questions that, when answered, can provide valuable input to the decisions we make—and the culture we create—around the ever-present issue of failure. (See the sidebar "Responding to Failure.")

Recovery time from a failure will vary, depending on the severity of the problem and the personality of the employee. Again, avoid a witch hunt mentality or assigning blame, and do assist with a confidence reboot. Studies suggest that women struggle more with confidence after a fail

Responding to Failure

When an employee or team has experienced a major misstep, try this exercise to understand, bounce back from, and make the most of failure:

1. Begin with why the failure happened. What process was not in place or could be improved?

2. Was the failure a result of lack of effort or due to trying something new and having it not work?

3. Is this person or team failing because they are in the wrong role(s)?

4. Are unrealistic expectations partly to blame for the failure? Could expectations be managed differently?

5. How quickly will you recover from this failure? What important truths did you learn from this experience? Meaning, now that you've invested in this mistake, what kind of return will there be for your organization?

than men, partly because human beings have a tendency to judge men on potential and women on track record.[6] We also judge women's failures more harshly than men's and remember them for longer.[7] A blot on the record can hit hard and make it difficult to rebound.

Harvard Business School's Amy Edmondson has studied failure extensively, from NASA space shuttle explosions to mining disasters to hospital accidents. Her analysis is that responding wisely to failure is exactly how companies become "learning organizations" and avoid future catastrophes. "Failure is not always bad," she writes in her 2011 article "Strategies for Learning from Failure." "In organizational life it is sometimes bad, sometimes inevitable, and sometimes even good."[8] But as people become masters, they get out of practice at failing—it starts to feel scary and threatening in a way that it didn't when they were beginners.

Techniques to aid in recovery should be in the toolbox of every manager. Like encouraging your employees to embrace mistakes. Jeff Michalski, founder of famed comedy club the Second City, told comedian Stephen Colbert and his other improvisation students, "You have to learn to love the bomb." Colbert explains further: "It took me a long time to really understand what that meant. It wasn't 'Don't worry, you'll get it next time.' It wasn't 'Laugh it off.' No, it means what it says. You gotta learn to love when you're failing . . . The embracing of that, the discomfort of failing in front of an audience, leads you to penetrate through the fear that blinds you."[9]

You may not learn to love watching your employees bomb, but you can learn to value failure for the education it can provide. You can see it as the price of taking the risks required to venture onto the frontier of a new learning curve. And you can come to handle it sensitively and help them reap the benefits that a resounding failure can produce.

On the Cusp

In chemistry, when a reacting atom or molecule stands at the top of the mountain between one chemical state and another (like from water to steam), it is part of what's called a "transition complex."[10] A transition complex is a combination of all the particles involved in a reaction. They are unstable, but for a brief instant, they act as one.

As with a chemical reaction, an employee at the top of the curve is in a state of transition. Will they regress, sliding down the curve into complacency? Or progress, bringing others along the curve, before they jump to a new one? You help inform this choice. Your employee is waiting for you to provide a seedbed for the germination and blossoming of their talent. They want opportunities to beef up their skill set, keep them relevant, and add value to their career portfolio. They want big, meaningful problems to solve. They want to contribute. Your high-enders can still be part of your A-team, but if you make the mistake of managing them as if they are still in the sweet spot of the learning curve, they may fall into the precipice.

Summary

- At the top of the S curve, progress levels out. Boredom and stagnation can lead to lower productivity and a loss of human resource value.

- Some employees will actively seek a new opportunity. Others may enjoy the comfort of their position and lack the motivation to jump. There are managerial techniques available to help in both situations as well as those that fall between the extremes.

- While high-enders (roughly 15 percent of your employees) are waiting to jump to a new curve, deploy them as pacesetters, trainers, and mentors to those at the low end of the curve.

- Failure is inevitable. Manage it well, and it can become a powerful tool for progress. Be a force for changing the corporate culture around failure when necessary.

HELPING PEOPLE LEAP TO NEW LEARNING CURVES

You are like this cup; you are full of ideas. You come and
ask for teaching, but your cup is full; I can't put anything in.
Before I can teach you, you'll have to empty your cup.

—Zen teaching, paraphrased, from Zen master Ryutan

A learning curve can be compared to the seasons of the year: a
new beginning sprouting in spring, the tipping point reached
with rapid growth and productivity for summer, the graceful
slowdown of fall, and the inevitable yielding to the frozen winter at the very top of the curve. Without a subsequent spring—a
new curve for growth to begin again—employees get stuck in a
Groundhog Day scenario, in which they repeat the same snowy
day over and over again. Many highly proficient workers are
living a version of Bill Murray's endlessly repeated day. You have
a choice: You can leave them in place and watch them suffer a

gradual, even precipitous, decline in productivity; you can watch them abruptly depart for a warmer professional climate. Or, you can find a new learning curve for them to climb.

Kara Goldin, founder and CEO of Hint Inc., secured a place on the shelves at her local Whole Foods for her flagship product—fruit-flavored, sugar- and additive-free Hint Water—before she'd even developed it. She dropped the first cases off on her way to the hospital to give birth to her fourth child. That was in 2005. Today, Hint is a $100 million-a-year business.

Goldin understands that the time for an employee to look around for their next mountain to climb is not *after* they've become bored and complacent and their performance has slipped, but before. For example, one of her senior employees had been working with the COO on supply chain issues and sustainability. When Goldin asked if he was happy, he said he loved what he was doing. Goldin shared with me, "I told him to hire someone to replace himself." "What are you talking about?" he asked. Goldin then reminded him that the company wasn't growing at 5 or 10 percent per year; it was growing at 80 to 100 percent. "You should be saying to the senior executive team, 'Here's my plan: I'm getting to the top of the mountain, and I'm happy with what I'm doing, but I want to train my replacement because, for my next level of development, it's time to look for new opportunities.'" Goldin teaches her employees to go to their superiors and start the conversation. She wants them to say, "Listen, I love and enjoy my job. I feel like I'm performing really well, but what else can I do?"

As we know from past chapters, one of the most powerful ways managers can foster innovation in their teams and engagement in their people is to keep them moving to new learning curves before they get bored. Taking charge around the who, what, when, where, and how of these leaps is critical. Should your people proactively lobby for a jump to a new curve when they reach the top? Yes. But remember, it's a lot harder for them to come to you and say "I'm at the top of my curve, I need to try something new" than you think it is. The boss holds most of the cards in this situation, and an employee may feel that asking to jump is tantamount to asking for a push into unemployment.[1] You hold the power: Is the top of the curve a place where people decide to leave because they know there's nothing more? Is it a spot where they outlive their usefulness and become organizational deadweight? Or, is it the launching pad for even greater effectiveness?

Come to Their AID

If you haven't already, it's time to sit down with your high-performing employee and work with them to figure out their next move. During the employee's ascent up the present curve, you have gathered and analyzed data as part of the discovery-driven process of disruption. You've used this data to calibrate performance and maximize their success throughout the sweet spot. At the high end of the curve, this discovery achieved critical mass and has been utilized to congratulate them on what they have achieved and what they want to learn and do in the future.

Now that you've determined your employee has or is about to top out on their current learning curve, it's time to come to their AID. This is a three-step process:

1. **A**pplaud their achievements.

2. **I**dentify a new learning curve.

3. **D**eliver on helping them jump.

Applaud

Review what your employee has accomplished. Recognize them for it, like you would for someone graduating from college. Give them the opportunity to bask in their accomplishments and celebrate. At the beginning of this learning curve, you asked what needed to happen for this person to achieve their potential, and this helped reverse engineer their success. Now evaluate what has happened because they were in this role. What abilities—both their acquired skills and their native gifts, or superpowers—helped them excel? How and why have they succeeded? Applaud them for their performance.

Identify

Talk openly with your star performer about the concept of the S-shaped learning curve. Explain that when mastery is reached, they will be on the brink of a new opportunity.

Work with them to identify opportunities in-house that they might be interested in pursuing. What is the reasonable next step that aligns with the experience they've gained? What are the goals they have in mind? What kinds of challenges do you think, and do they think, would keep them innovating and producing? Make a commitment to help them jump to a new curve within six to nine months. Let them know that soon their restless brain will be at the bottom of a new curve with lots of room for growth. Ask them to commit in return to a strong finish in their current role.

You may have had a plan in mind for this employee's next step, back when they first came on board at the low end of the curve. But through the process of discovery over several years of employment, both the employee and their circumstances have changed. During that time, the firm has changed, too, ever evolving to remain competitive in a business climate that is also continuously changing. The original plan may no longer be feasible, or it may not be advantageous to either your employee or the business. But if you're maintaining a discovery-driven mindset, you can make the most of your employee, regardless of what's changed.

Deliver

Facilitating the jump to a new curve can feel risky; managers face the prospect of a giant hole on their team and a consequent loss of productivity. But they will face this prospect anyway if their talent roams away in search of greener pastures.

When you put the interests of your employees first, you serve your own best interests. Deliver on the promise inherent in your relationship: They've given their all toward the team's success. Now help them jump to a new curve where they can continue to succeed. The central issue is trust. If your people trust that you want to help them achieve their goals and have a stake in their interests, they will reciprocate by sharing those goals with you and giving their best effort. This kind of openness is often absent in cutthroat cultures, but it can be achieved.

Putting employee development first will almost never benefit you in the short term, but over the long term, it will. Expand your time horizon. It will be easier to create the spirit of mutual trust essential to the process of personal disruption. And remember Newton's third law: for every action, there is an equal and opposite reaction. In chapter 5, we talked about this in the context of giving sweet-spotters assignments that would stretch them. Now, let's flip it a bit. Instead of thinking about pushing against, just think push. Like pushing people to jump to a new learning curve. When you hoard talent, you pull in, you take. When you develop people, you push them—and you—forward. What you give, you will eventually get back.

Consider Lateral Moves

The goal is always to retain talent, but the more people achieve seniority, the more it becomes a challenge. Not everyone can go up. But it is also true that "up" isn't the only way up: a lot of learning and growth can happen in lateral moves that may eventually give employees the perfect skill set to forge ahead.

In corporate legal departments, people tend to stay in the same job for a long time. Not Ruby Zefo, VP and chief privacy and security counsel at Intel. She arrived at Intel in 2003 to manage the Trademark group. Over time she added to her responsibilities, seeking tasks outside her wheelhouse. She then picked up corporate affairs and the Intel Foundation, Intel's nonprofit subsidiary that covers corporate responsibility, grant making, science fairs, and women-to-girl outreach initiatives, where the legal challenges were not that obvious. "It was the best group I've ever supported," she says. "Everything was a celebration."

After scaling this curve, Zefo handed the responsibility off to a successor, and she was ready for a new challenge. In 2011 her boss, Suzan Miller, looked at Intel's product roadmap and decided they needed someone to build a legal department around data privacy and security and who could offer more-strategic, senior support to the IT department. Miller felt the position would require a leap of faith—but she knew that Zefo knew how to build global teams and could figure it out. Zefo took on the opportunity, even though she knew very little about the topic. It required a major deep dive from a legal content and practice perspective. "I had to do while I learned. I read everything I could, went to every local conference, expanded my network, used outside counsel. It was an enormous amount of effort, until one day I realized I knew as much as the person on the stage." It was this job that catapulted her to a coveted VP spot and earned her a seat on the board of the International Association of Privacy Professionals.

Now Zefo continues to learn and grow by tackling the messiness of new technologies that are running ahead of legislation and sometimes even ethics (providing legal support to Intel's new Artificial Intelligence Products Group, for example).

This is the trajectory that ambitious professionals aspire to. If they have an opportunity to build personal equity with your firm, it is likely they will. If they don't get the chance, they'll become dried up or fed up.

A lateral move may be the best (or only) option for an employee to jump to a new learning curve in-house, but it's one that may have undesirable consequences for their status or paycheck. Finding an elegant solution when it would seem the only way up is up requires creativity. Compensation expert Stacey Petrey encourages managers to have a candid conversation with the potential curve jumper. She suggests asking, "'What are you willing to trade off in exchange for a new curve?' Flexibility? Being co-lead, rather than lead on a project? Once you've figured this out, you can solve the problem of pay. Don't ask them to give up title or base pay. It's hard to recover from a drop in either." Don't let them negotiate against themselves. Women in particular tend to negotiate away their value too readily. Says Petrey: "Giving a lot up isn't seen as a sign of good faith but of weakness."[2]

Consider Backward Moves

If lateral moves carry some stigma, then backward moves are often seen as even more of a head-scratcher. We tend to assume something's wrong with someone who takes a step back. But sometimes taking a step back is exactly the right move. Like the slingshot, we pull back to get the momentum we need to catapult forward.

In 2013, Dan Shapero was one of twenty-five VPs at LinkedIn and global head of sales. He'd started in operations in 2008, when LinkedIn was a six-hundred-person organization. Since then, they'd grown tenfold. In 2010, he was given a stretch assignment: move into sales, which at the time was new to him. He started with a team of eight people and revenue of $40 million. Three years later, Shapero had grown revenue to $1 billion and was leading the largest business unit at the company, with a team of a thousand. He was on a tear. According to Mike Gamson, now senior VP of global solutions and Shapero's boss at the time, "Dan had gone as far as you can go in the sales track by running the biggest line we have."

What was next? During a walking meeting with his boss's boss, CEO Jeff Weiner, Shapero shared his dream of becoming a tech CEO. Weiner's response was, "If you want to lead a tech company, you're in the wrong job." Not the victory lap conversation Shapero was hoping for. He'd built the business, helped the company scale, and was now discovering he couldn't get there from here. After a brief bout of frustration and two months of deliberation, Shapero went to Gamson and Weiner and said, "Let's do it. Let's build great tech products." *Say what?* Shapero was a VP, a sales leader with a thousand reports, generating a billion in revenue, and he wanted to move to product management. This led to a discussion about what was best for LinkedIn. And questions about the time horizon. "Dan was willing to suboptimize the sub-system to optimize the system," says Gamson.

Based on data that LinkedIn had access to (and they had a lot), few, if any, employees moved from sales to product. It would be a radical leap for Shapero, and they would receive pushback, starting with the senior executives. Shapero was good at sales, and people had pigeonholed him as a sales guy. So the CEO's input was especially important. "Our CEO, Jeff, was very open," Gamson recalls. "He was very nondogmatic about what makes a product person. It's not, 'Are you a product person or are you not?' He had a growth mindset. This allowed for the sponsorship to be effective."

When I asked Gamson how he felt about losing Shapero, his response surprised me. "Delighted. The best people in the world can do almost anything they want. I can promise to create a trajectory-changing experience for them. And I get loyalty. Or I can play, 'What can you do for me now?' and have the best people leave. The company wins when I put the company next."

Shapero moved to product, not as a leader but as an individual contributor, working with three engineers. He had no direct reports and no promises of any career path. He reported to Kevin Simon, senior director of product. Simon had been two levels below Shapero, but now he was Shapero's boss. Simon admits that he had mixed feelings. On the one hand, "I was excited. It was a bit like playing in little league and having a major league player join your team." Also, he continues, "Because Dan had absolutely no product experience, he was going to bring a fresh perspective, a diversity of thought to the team . . . But, it was a little intimidating. Managing someone with more experience, more seniority, and a strong relationship with the CEO was unnerving."

There was also the challenge of managing the team dynamics. Simon had people on his team who had been project managers for a long time. There were people who'd been passed over for promotion due to a lack of experience. "It's like having a new child in the family. How do you make sure all the kids are getting the attention?"

The actual onboarding was fairly simple. LinkedIn brings people on all the time with no experience. During his first six months on the job, "Half the work I felt amazing at; half I was terrible at," Shapero says. Simon coached him and gave him a buddy/mentor, like everyone else gets. Except it was different. "At the same time Dan was onboarding, he was contributing at ten times the level of his title." That was true in part because he was figuring out a way to play where LinkedIn's competitors weren't—by building products for job seekers. Before long, this became one of the fastest-growing product areas on the site.

Fast-forward to 2016, when Shapero became VP of LinkedIn's $2 billion talent solutions and careers business

Stepping Sideways or Back as a Slingshot

Moving an employee from one department or team to another, either laterally or as a step back, can feel like a risky proposition. Discuss the following questions with your employee to assess whether such a move has the potential to become a slingshot.

- What is your ultimate career goal or dream? Can you get there on the track you're on, or will it require experience, skills, or knowledge gained on a different track?

- What is it you want to learn? Where inside the organization can you learn it? How will the knowledge you already have benefit another department or team?

- How difficult will it be to learn a new skill set, department, or industry? Are you willing to be a novice again?

line, which has both sales and marketing, his former business unit, and product reporting into him.

Shapero's step back became a slingshot. "It worked because Dan approached this with absolutely no ego," says Simon. He was even willing to accept a small decline in compensation. "[Taking a step back] was an incredibly rare thing to do. But it yielded a ton of value." It also worked because Gamson, his sponsoring boss in sales, and Simon, his boss in product, were willing to make it work, while CEO Jeff Weiner expected it to work. There was also help from the head of HR, Pat Wadors, and internal executive coach Fred Kofman.

Shapero took a gargantuan risk to disrupt his own career path (something he'd seen his parents do: his dad moved from business to law in his fifties, his mother from retail to psychology in her forties). But without the go-ahead and support from multiple management pieces, the disruption would have been a no-go. (See the sidebar "Stepping Sideways or Back as a Slingshot.")

Shake Things Up

Thinking creatively may reveal potential personnel moves that can make sense both for the employee and the company. During her tenure at Rovi, a 2,500-employee digital media software and service company, Eileen Schloss, who was then chief human resource officer, realized that two of her HR teams had become locked in conflict: HR business partners (HRBP), the team that guides leaders through employee challenges and organizational design, and global talent acquisition, which is responsible for hiring. "The HR business partners tended to complain that jobs weren't getting filled fast enough for their client managers," says Schloss. "The talent people felt the HRBP people didn't adequately convey to the client managers what it takes to fill a role."

Greasing the Wheels of Disruption

Managing people as a series of S curves requires a disruptive mindset on your part. Here are some important questions to consider.

- How can I shake up employees or teams who have become set in their ways?

- What goals might be accomplished by shifting people into different roles?

- How can I create a company culture that encourages and even insists on curve jumping?

She asked the heads of each team to trade places. "This forced switch in perspective made a huge difference," says Schloss. "Neither of them initially had the experience to perform their new job, but they had the knowledge of the business generally, and they had people working for them who understood the specifics. This purposeful shakeup improved understanding within each function, as well as capabilities."

Moreover, it gave each executive new skills. When one of them, Zoe Harte, later became VP and head of HR at jobs site Upwork, Schloss says "she sent me some flowers and thanked me for my support and for pushing her to try new things." By suggesting, and sometimes even imposing new S curves to climb, managers can help good employees grow into great ones. (See the sidebar "Greasing the Wheels of Disruption.")

As CEO of Hershey Resorts and Entertainment, Bill Simpson had a tough decision to make. He had two great candidates for an open role but could only promote one of them.

With more than 1,500 full-time employees, Hershey Resorts in Hershey, Pennsylvania, is a collection of properties and conference facilities and an amusement park full of candy-themed rides. It's also an organization that drills down on succession planning. "I have a notebook on the top seventy managers in the organization," says Simpson. "Every year I report on them to the board. We try to promote from within 50 percent of the time."

The general manager (GM) for Hershey Lodge was retiring after forty years with the company. A replacement was needed for their largest hotel, a 665-room property with 100,000 square feet of meeting space. There were two front-runners. One knew revenue management, client relations, and contract administration. The other knew hotel operations. In the end, Simpson appointed the former to the GM spot and promoted the latter to assistant GM under him.

Simpson knew the new assistant GM would likely be disappointed at not making the top spot, and also that he had the potential to be a great GM someday. So the company made a promise to him: when the GM spot at another major property, the Hotel Hershey, came up, management wouldn't go to market but would promote him instead.

This may also happen to you. You don't have the right role for someone at the right time. Be transparent, both about your commitment to them and their prospects with the company. Six months later, the GM of Hotel Hershey retired. "It was important that we keep our word," says Simpson. "Anybody can build a taller roller coaster. But the experience of our guests is built by people. We win on people."

Where to Climb When You're at the Top

What if you are at the top of the curve and on top at your company: the CEO or another position in the C-suite? CEOs occupy a unique and rarefied niche of fiduciary responsibility to governing boards and, in the case of public companies, to shareholders. The initiatives that must be undertaken to fulfill this responsibility have an S curve of their own and may take some time to bear fruit.

In fact, the average tenure of a CEO at the largest 500 US companies is 4.9 years.[3] There are notable exceptions to the brief tenure: Warren Buffett, for example, has led Berkshire Hathaway for 59 years, and Rupert Murdoch has been CEO of News Corp for 63. *Fortune* 500 companies have a slightly longer average CEO tenure of 7.4 years, but analysts point to guys like Buffett and Murdoch as the reason it's that long.[4] Most CEOs seem to move on, voluntarily or not, within five years.

There is a lot to learn at this level. There are multiple domains to understand as well as the myriad nuances of a specific enterprise and its markets. Some find it can provide an ongoing challenge over several decades. Garry Ridge, CEO of WD-40 Company, has been in place for more than twenty years, and the company's numbers are stellar. If that changes, the board will show him the door. In the meantime, he engages in ongoing education, coaching, writing, opening new markets, and expanding the offerings of what was, for a long time, a single product company. He disrupts himself and stays relevant.

Those who helm a company they founded or own may be in the toughest spot (see the sidebar "The Final Curve"). Without the guidance of a board or the accountability to shareholders, the responsibility falls on individual shoulders to determine when and how to disrupt oneself. Maybe you have a great idea but not necessarily the education or acumen to run a business—a very steep learning curve that is likely to take some time to surf. To ensure that personal growth is a priority along with growing the business, I advise investing in coaching.

Because CEOs, and C-suiters in general, are people too and subject to boredom, if you don't disrupt yourself, someone is likely to do it for you. Marshall Goldsmith, who has coached more than 150 CEOs, advises clients, "It's better to stay one year too short than one day too long. Don't overstay your welcome. As a CEO, set a certain time, make your contribution and leave. Don't hang on. And be developing your successor . . . Leave with style and dignity, and leave on your own terms . . . You're a CEO ten years? You're throwing the dice."[5]

The Final Curve

For some employees, there may not be a next curve to jump to within the organization. I think especially of late-career professionals who are approaching semi- or full retirement. The data tells us that more and more people are choosing—or are forced—to work past traditional retirement milestones. While some may be interested and feel they have the work-life bandwidth remaining to tackle entirely new learning curves, others may not.

Mentorship and training roles are especially good ways to deploy these experienced employees who are veritable libraries of domain- and firm-specific expertise and memory. Reasonable efforts to accommodate their needs—perhaps they want to work part-time or remotely to allow for travel—can keep them contributing at great benefit to everyone involved. Many will be willing to discuss adjustments to compensation that will maintain their high value to the firm while allowing them more flexibility to pursue noncareer objectives. The key is to think creatively. Years of experience is a human resource not to be wasted.

Summary

- As with other investments, the time comes to rebalance the portfolio by helping a top-end employee disrupt to a new learning curve.

- Most disruptions require management facilitation. High-end performers may desire a new curve but can't get there on their own. This is where you can come to their AID: *applaud* their achievements, *identify* a new learning curve, *deliver* on helping them jump.

- Facilitating your employee's jump to a new curve requires battling entitlement—in yourself, as well as your employee.

- New S curves for people stimulate innovation for companies. Think creatively about how to slingshot your people in new directions.

CONCLUSION

GETTING STARTED

We are very near to greatness: one step and we are safe: can we not take the leap?

—Ralph Waldo Emerson

It makes no sense to have your best, brightest, and most-experienced employees leave to pursue opportunities elsewhere because they are bored. Yet too many companies make exactly this mistake.

Boris Groysberg, a professor of organizational behavior at Harvard Business School, has administered a "Building a Great Company" survey to small- and medium-sized companies around the globe for the past decade, asking questions about topics ranging from strategy to culture. He asks executives to rate "How effective is your company" on thirty-seven HR practices, from recruitment to engagement. For the 450 companies surveyed in 2017, "job rotations" had the lowest rating, with "high-potential program" coming in at third lowest. "This was not unusual," Groysberg notes. "These practices have long been at the bottom of the list." Clearly many companies struggle to provide employees at the top of their learning curve with new assignments and opportunities internally.

The ability for managers to support their employees through a series of learning curves requires a willingness to stretch beyond the parameters of everyday thinking. It also requires that managers have the support of upper management. But this requires change. And change, as we all know, can be tough for organizations to handle. We talk a good game, but the reality of our human condition is that few of us like "new" until it's no longer new. We prefer the sure thing, the familiar status quo that has brought us to our present level of success. Stasis provides a semblance of certainty and safety. Except that really, safety and certainty are an illusion.

In risk-averse organizations, it may be hard to convince your superiors that it's a good idea to move a star employee to a new role where their success is far from guaranteed. It may be difficult to make the case for hiring someone with more potential than experience. It may feel impossible to get buy-in for the idea that an employee who is underperforming in one role could be a standout in a different role.

If your company is the kind of organization that tends to point out what could go wrong, you will not convince anyone to change by arguing that managing employees in a new way will unlock innovation, feelings of achievement and satisfaction, and engagement. If your company has a glass-half-empty way of looking at things, then work with their risk-averse survival instinct rather than against it. Make it scarier *not* to try something new.

Lay out the risks of *not* encouraging people to disrupt themselves: what it could cost you, your boss, your team, and your company. Here are some points to bring up:

- You will lose your high potentials. You can't continue to "like them right where they are," because they won't stay. If you don't help broker in-house moves to keep them stretching, they'll broker their own move to a new employer.

- Even if they do stay, if you don't push people into challenging, constrained situations, they won't be engaged.

- If they aren't engaged, they won't innovate. (They may not even really work.)

- If they don't innovate, your company will become less competitive. You will be beaten by faster-adapting competitors because you won't be prepared for the future. According to an in-depth study conducted by Accenture, high-performing companies (those that surpass their peers on financial metrics across business cycles and leadership eras) are those that develop capabilities *before* they need them. Average and low-performing companies don't, which is why they can't compete.[1]

Want to know if you're about to be disrupted? Take the pulse of your workforce. Says writer Anne Lamott: "If we stay where we are, where we're stuck, where we're comfortable and safe, we die there. We become like mushrooms, living in the dark, with poop up to our chins. If you want to know only what you already know, you're dying."[2]

That said, don't argue that the learning-curve approach to management has no downsides—it's just that the upsides far outweigh them. For instance, if you help talented employees jump to new roles, yes, your team may suffer in the short term. But in the long term, you will gain a reputation as a talent developer. Capable, ambitious, high-potential people will want to work for you.

If you hire someone who isn't already an expert, you'll also have lower productivity for a time. That person won't be able to just plug right into the role. But they will be happy to have the job and be loyal to you, since you took a chance on them. They will be eager to work hard and prove themselves. Your entire team will benefit from this highly engaged employee. This approach entails some risk—but not as much risk as sticking with the status quo.

Remember that for yourself, too. Because the most frequent reservation people have about allowing their subordinates to disrupt themselves through successive learning curves is this: concern that their superiors won't support this new paradigm, that they won't reward and may even punish them for trying it.

But in my experience, the biggest obstacle to this management style is not the higher-ups. There's always a higher-up,

even when you are the CEO. It starts with the person reading or listening to this book. The single biggest impediment
to innovation in your organization could be *you*.

Whether you oversee a team of ten or ten thousand, remember
that you are positioned to help others. You can reward and
promote them and aid their personal disruptions. I'm sure you
want to do that, or you wouldn't have bought this book—and
made it this far. But helping others learn and grow is always
the kind of thing that seems easier to do tomorrow. It's easy
to say, "Today I'm just too busy." Or "This quarter is not the
time to move my best employee to a new role."

The best bosses don't just build one A-team; they build
vast networks of A-teams over the course of their careers.
Generosity and assistance bring long-term rewards. As you
facilitate and celebrate the success of others, it will burnish
your reputation as a talent developer and a boss who people
love to work for.

A manager, like a coach, must know that you don't win
unless your team does. As you aspire to be a boss who leads
their team up the learning curve, be patient with yourself
and with others. People often say to me, "Your ideas are
terrific, but it all comes down to execution." It does. But our
fear of not executing brilliantly can leave us stranded at the
starting line, unwilling to even try.

One of the great examples of being willing to start, make
mistakes, and then patiently course-correct is Benjamin
Franklin. He wanted to achieve moral perfection. He made
a list of thirteen virtues. But he didn't try to master them
all at once. Instead he "executed" one at a time, beginning

with temperance, because a cool head was foundational to the remaining twelve virtues, which also included industry, moderation, and humility. He wrestled with these goals throughout his life, giving focused practice to each of the thirteen for a week and then beginning the cycle anew. He said, "Having a garden to weed, [one] does not attempt to eradicate all the bad herbs at once, but works on the beds one at a time . . ." As you learn to disrupt yourself, and help others do the same, work on one bed at a time. On discouraging days, take heart from Franklin's wisdom when he said, "A perfect character might be attended with the inconvenience of being envied or hated. A benevolent man should allow a few faults in himself, to keep his friends in countenance."[3]

Throughout this book, I have extolled the value of constraints: in fostering creativity and in forcing action. As a manager of people, remember that of all the constraints we face, time is the most unyielding. Other resources may multiply, but time is always finite. Whether it's our time in a job or our time on this planet, the amount of time we have left is always shrinking.

We are driven forward by our consciousness of limited time. It is a force more potent than the need to have a job or to earn a paycheck. People want to dream, and then they want to realize their dreams by learning new things, developing new competencies, and having an opportunity to make an imprint on the world. Managers can be makers, generating opportunities for their team members to create and recreate themselves through personal disruption.[4] What a wonderful day's work that would be.

NOTES

Introduction

1. "WD-40 Company History," Funding Universe, accessed November 17, 2017, http://www.fundinguniverse.com/company-histories/wd-40-company-history/.

2. Larry Emond, "2 Reasons Why Employee Engagement Programs Fall Short," Gallup News, August 15, 2007, http://news.gallup.com/opinion/gallup/216155/reasons-why-employee-engagement-programs-fall-short.aspx.

3. Whitney Johnson, interview with Garry Ridge, *Disrupt Yourself* podcast, episode 13, March 10, 2017, https://soundcloud.com/disruptyourselfpodcast/episode-13-garry-ridge.

4. Ibid.

5. Marissa Brassfield, "Study Reveals Majority of Workers Feel Trapped in Their Jobs," PayScale Career News page, July 2013, https://www.payscale.com/career-news/2013/07/study-reveals-majority-of-workers-feel-trapped-in-their-jobs.

6. Erin Werthman, "Survey Says: American Workers Are Stuck in a Rut," Rasmussen College, April 15, 2014, http://www.rasmussen.edu/press-release/2014-04-15/survey-says-american-workers-stuck-in-a-rut/.

7. "U.S. Luxury Car Market Share in 2016, by Brand," Statista, 2017, https://www.statista.com/statistics/287620/luxury-vehicles-united-states-premium-vehicle-market-share/.

Chapter 1

1. Tony Horwitz, *Blue Latitudes: Boldly Going Where Captain Cook Has Gone Before*, reprint edition (New York: Henry Holt and Co., 2003), 290–292, 297, 304–307, 316–317.

2. "The Millennial Economy," a survey of 1,200 millennials conducted by public policy organization Economic Innovation Group, http://eig.org/millennial.

3. Beth Kowitt, "Why McDonald's Wins in Any Economy," *Fortune*, September 5, 2011.

4. Seminar with Alan Mulally, Marshall Goldsmith 100 Coaches conference, Phoenix, AZ, December 2016.

5. Whitney Johnson, interview with Bernie Swain, *Disrupt Yourself* podcast, episode 8, December 29, 2016, http://whitneyjohnson.com/bernie-swain-disrupt-yourself.

6. Antony Jay, *Machiavelli and Management: An Inquiry into the Politics of Corporate Life* (San Diego: Pfeiffer & Co, 1994), 45, 71–72.

Chapter 2

1. Whitney Johnson, interview with Sarah Feingold, *Disrupt Yourself* podcast, episode 7, December 14, 2016, https://soundcloud.com/disruptyourselfpodcast/episode-07-sarah-feingold.

2. Whitney Johnson, *Disrupt Yourself: Putting the Power of Disruptive Innovation to Work* (New York: Bibliomotion, 2015), 10–11.

3. Whitney Johnson, interview with Walter O'Brien, *Disrupt Yourself* podcast, episode 29, October 12, 2017, https://soundcloud.com/disruptyourselfpodcast/episode-29-walter-obrien.

4. Pierre Chandon, "The Reason We Buy (and Eat) Too Much Food," *Harvard Business Review*, December 20, 2016, https://hbr.org/2016/12/the-reasons-we-buy-and-eat-too-much-food.

5. Liz Wiseman, *Rookie Smarts* (New York: HarperBusiness, 2014), 1–3.

6. Whitney Johnson, interview with Raju Narisetti, *Disrupt Yourself* podcast, episode 2, October 6, 2016, https://soundcloud.com/disruptyourselfpodcast/episode-02-raju-narisetti.

7. Jack Zenger and Joseph Folkman, "Why Do So Many Managers Avoid Giving Praise?" *Harvard Business Review*, May 2, 2017, https://hbr.org/2017/05/why-do-so-many-managers-avoid-giving-praise.

8. Marcel Schwantes, "Want to Totally Transform Your Leadership? Give This to Your Employees Once Per Week," Inc.com, November 22, 2016, https://www.inc.com/marcel-schwantes/research-says-this-absurdly-simple-habit-is-a-powerful-way-to-get-employees-moti.html.

9. Gretchen Rubin, *The Happiness Project: Or, Why I Spent a Year Trying to Sing in the Morning, Clean My Closets, Fight Right, Read Aristotle, and Generally Have More Fun*, revised edition (New York: HarperCollins, 2015), 268.

10. Whitney Johnson, interview with Michelle McKenna-Doyle, *Disrupt Yourself* podcast, episode 1, September 23, 2016, https://soundcloud.com/disruptyourselfpodcast/episode-01-michelle-mckenna-doyle.

11. Sam Pitroda with David Chanoff, *Dreaming Big: My Journey to Connect India* (Oakbrook Terrace, IL: The Pitroda Group, 2015), 144–145.

12. Jean Martin and Conrad Schmidt, "How to Keep Your Top Talent," *Harvard Business Review*, May 2010, https://hbr.org/2010/05/how-to-keep-your-top-talent.

13. Johnson, *Disrupt Yourself*, 112–114.

14. Jody Genessy, "Big Questions Loom About Jazz Rotations as Playoffs Approach," Deseret News.com, March 30, 2017, http://www.deseretnews.com/article/865676786/Big-questions-loom-about-Jazz-rotations-as-playoffs-approach.html.

15. Marguerite Ward, "This Biz Bounced Back from Near Failure to Sell Over 1 Million Products," CNBC.com "Make It" page, May 25, 2016, http://www.cnbc.com/2016/05/25/this-biz-bounced-back-from-near-failure-to-sell-over-1-million-products.html.

Chapter 3

1. Tara Sophia Mohr, "The Real Reason Women Don't Apply for Jobs Unless They're 100% Qualified," *Harvard Business Review*, August 24, 2014, https://hbr.org/2014/08/why-women-dont-apply-for-jobs-unless-theyre-100-qualified.

2. Adam Vaccaro, "Why Employees Quit Jobs Right After They've Started," Inc.com, April 17, 2014, http://www.inc.com/adam-vaccaro/voluntary-turnover-six-months.html.

3. Eileen Appelbaum and Ruth Milkman, *Achieving a Workable Balance: New Jersey Employers' Experiences Managing Employee Leaves and Turnover* (New Brunswick, NJ: Center for Women and Work, 2006).

4. David Rosnick, "How Much Does Employee Turnover Really Cost Your Business?" Center for Economic and Policy Research, CLASP-CEPR Turnover Calculator, http://cepr.net/research-tools/online-calculators/clasp-cepr-turnover-calculator.

5. Heather Boushey and Sarah Jane Glynn, "There Are Significant Business Costs to Replacing Employees," Center for American Progress, November 16, 2012, https://www.americanprogress.org/wp-content/uploads/2012/11/CostofTurnover.pdf.

6. Whitney Johnson, interview with Patrick Pichette, *Disrupt Yourself* podcast, episode 10, January 26, 2017, https://soundcloud.com/disruptyourselfpodcast/episode-10-patrick-pichette.

7. Victoria Luby and Jane Stevenson, "7 Tenets of a Good CEO Succession Process," *Harvard Business Review*, December 7, 2016, https://hbr.org/2016/12/7-tenets-of-a-good-ceo-succession-process.

8. Dave Winsborough, "It's Common for Peers to Punish Top Performers in High-Performing Teams," LinkedIn, July 10, 2017, https://www.linkedin.com/pulse/its-common-peers-punish-top-performers-high-teams-dave-winsborough.

9. Dave Winsborough and Tomas Chamorro-Premuzic, "Great Teams Are About Personalities, Not Just Skills," *Harvard Business Review*, January 25, 2017, https://hbr.org/2017/01/great-teams-are-about-personalities-not-just-skills?utm_campaign=hbr&utm_source=twitter&utm_medium=social.

10. A.G. Lafley and Roger L. Martin, "Customer Loyalty Is Overrated," *Harvard Business Review*, January–February 2017, https://hbr.org/2017/01/customer-loyalty-is-overrated.

11. Whitney Johnson, *Disrupt Yourself*, 3.

12. Drake Baer, "Hiring, Like Dating, Sucks; Here's How Startups Are Trying to Fix It," *Fast Company*, February 28, 2013, https://www.fastcompany.com/3006365/hiring-dating-sucks-heres-how-startups-are-trying-fix-it.

13. Author's email interview with Lauren Rivera, July 11, 2017.

14. Benjamin Artz, Amanda Goodall, and Andrew J. Oswald, "If Your Boss Could Do Your Job, You're More Likely to Be Happy at Work," HBR.org, December 29, 2016, https://hbr.org/2016/12/if-your-boss-could-do-your-job-youre-more-likely-to-be-happy-at-work.

15. Dorothy Dalton, "A Plea! Keep Job Profiles Real!" Dorothy Dalton.com, December 1, 2010, http://dorothydalton.com/2010/12/01/a-plea-keep-job-profiles-real/.

16. Danielle Gaucher and Justin Friesen, "Evidence That Gendered Wording in Job Advertisements Exists and Sustains Gender Inequality," *Journal of Personality and Social Psychology* 101, no. 1 (2011): 109–128.

17. Claire Cain Miller, "Job Listings That Are Too 'Feminine' For Men," *New York Times*, January 16, 2017, https://www.nytimes.com/2017/01/16/upshot/job-disconnect-male-applicants-feminine-language.html.

18. Cliff Zukin and Mark Szeltner, "Talent Report: What Workers Want in 2012," Net Impact, through Rutgers University, May 2012, https://netimpact.org/sites/default/files/documents/what-workers-want-2012.pdf.

19. Erik Sherman, "35 Percent of All Workers Are Freelance? Not Quite," Inc.com, October 12, 2016, http://www.inc.com/erik-sherman/b35-percent-of-all-workers-are-freelance-not-quite/b.html.

20. Whitney Johnson, interview with Carol Fishman Cohen, July 20, 2017.

21. Gretchen Livingston, "Opting Out? About 10% of Highly Educated Moms Are Staying Home," Pew Research Center, May 7, 2014, http://www.pewresearch.org/fact-tank/2014/05/07/opting-out-about-10-of-highly-educated-moms-are-staying-at-home/.

22. Whitney Johnson, "What It's Like When a Stay-At-Home Dad Goes Back to Work," *Harvard Business Review*, April 19, 2016, https://hbr.org/2016/04/what-its-like-when-a-stay-at-home-dad-goes-back-to-work.

23. Michelle Weise, "We Need a Better Way to Visualize People's Skills," *Harvard Business Review*, September 20, 2016, https://hbr.org/2016/09/we-need-a-better-way-to-visualize-peoples-skills.

24. Whitney Johnson, interview with David Blake, August 16, 2017.

25. Steve Lohr, "A New Kind of Tech Job Emphasizes Skills, Not a College Degree," *New York Times*, June 28, 2017, https://www.nytimes.com/2017/06/28/technology/tech-jobs-skills-college-degree.html.

26. US Census Bureau, "Highest Educational Levels Reached by Adults in U.S. Since 1940," Census.gov, March 30, 2017, https://www.census.gov/newsroom/press-releases/2017/cb17-51.html.

27. Brian Rohrig, "Smartphones, Smart Chemistry," *ChemMatters*, April–May 2015, https://www.acs.org/content/acs/en/education/resources/highschool/chemmatters/past-issues/archive-2014-2015/smartphones.html.

Chapter 4

1. Whitney Johnson, interview with Don Cantore and John Gooch, audio recording, Lexington, VA, July 31, 2017 and August 2, 2017.

2. Inc.com, Global Partners' ranking on the Inc. 5000 page, 2017, https://www.inc.com/profile/globalization-partners.

3. Whitney Johnson, "You're Interviewing, and Pregnant," LinkedIn, November 26, 2013, https://www.linkedin.com/pulse/20131126192300-3414257-you-re-interviewing-and-pregnant?trk=pulse_spock-articles.

4. Heidi Grant Halvorson, *No One Understands You and What to Do About It* (Boston: Harvard Business Review Press, 2015), 12.

5. Janice Harper, "The Gentle Genocide of Workplace Mobbing," Just Us Justice, Academic Women for Justice.org, 2010, http://www.academicwomenforjustice.org/downloads/gentle-genocide.pdf.

6. David McCullough, *The Wright Brothers* (New York: Simon & Schuster, 2015), 116.

7. Eric Liu, *Guiding Lights: The People Who Lead Us Toward Our Purpose in Life* (New York: Random House, 2004), 57–62.

8. Carsten Wrosch, "Self-Regulation of Unattainable Goals and Pathways to Quality of Life" in *The Oxford Handbook of Stress, Health, and Coping*, edited by Susan Folkman (New York: Oxford University Press, 2011), 320.

9. "Surfers Only Spend 8% of the Time Riding Waves," *Surfer Today*, http://www.surfertoday.com/surfing/7653-surfers-only-spend-8-of-the-time-riding-waves.

10. Elder J. Devn Cornish, "Am I Good Enough? Will I Make It?" The Church of Jesus Christ of Latter-Day Saints, October 2016, https://www.lds.org/general-conference/2016/10/am-i-good-enough-will-i-make-it?lang=eng.

Chapter 5

1. Whitney Johnson, interview with Telisa Yancy, audio recording, Lexington, VA, August 2, 2017.

2. Amanda Imber, "Help Employees Innovate By Giving Them the Right Challenge," *Harvard Business Review*, October 17, 2016, https://hbr.org/2016/10/help-employees-innovate-by-giving-them-the-right-challenge.

3. Francesca Gino, "Are You Too Stressed to Be Productive? Or Not Stressed Enough?" *Harvard Business Review*, April 14, 2016, https://hbr.org/2016/04/are-you-too-stressed-to-be-productive-or-not-stressed-enough.

4. Jean Martin and Conrad Schmidt, "How to Keep Your Top Talent," *Harvard Business Review*, May 2010.

5. Alice Truong, "After Analyzing 200 Founders' Postmortems, Researchers Say These Are the Reasons Startups Fail," Quartz Media "Lesson Learned" page, May 12, 2016, https://qz.com/682517/after-analyzing-200-founders-postmortems-researchers-say-these-are-the-reasons-startups-fail/.

Chapter 6

1. Ron Chernow, *Alexander Hamilton* (New York: Penguin Books, 2004), 152.

2. Carol Hymowitz, "American Firms Want to Keep Older Workers a Bit Longer," *Bloomberg Businessweek*, December 16, 2016, https://www.bloomberg.com/news/articles/2016-12-16/american-firms-want-to-keep-older-workers-a-bit-longer.

3. Bryce G. Hoffman, *American Icon: Alan Mulally and the Fight to Save Ford Motor Company* (New York: Random House, 2012), 121.

4. J.P. Dunlon, "CEO of the Year Alan Mulally: The Road Ahead," *Chief Executive*, June 27, 2011, http://chiefexecutive.net/ceo-of-the-year-alan-mulally-the-road-ahead/.

5. Donald A. Schon, "Champions for Radical New Inventions," *Harvard Business Review*, March–April 1963.

6. Rosalind C. Barnett and Caryl Rivers, "How the 'New Discrimination' Is Holding Women Back," Catalyst, April 17, 2014, http://www.catalyst.org/zing/how-new-discrimination-holding-women-back.

7. Therese Huston, "Research: We Are Way Harder on Female Leaders Who Make Bad Calls," *Harvard Business Review*, April 21, 2016, https://hbr.org/2016/04/research-we-are-way-harder-on-female-leaders-who-make-bad-calls.

8. Amy C. Edmonson, "Strategies for Learning from Failure," *Harvard Business Review*, April 2011, https://hbr.org/2011/04/strategies-for-learning-from-failure.

9. Richard Feloni, "Stephen Colbert Shares the Best Lesson of His Career, Learned as an Improv Student at Second City," *Business Insider*, August 19, 2015, http://www.businessinsider.com/stephen-colbert-best-career-lesson-2015-8.

10. Henry J. Eyring, *Mormon Scientist: The Life and Faith of Henry Eyring* (Salt Lake City: Deseret Book, 2007), 27.

Chapter 7

1. Megan Reitz and John Higgins, "The Problem with Saying 'My Door Is Always Open,'" *Harvard Business Review*, March 9, 2017, https://hbr.org/2017/03/the-problem-with-saying-my-door-is-always-open.

2. Whitney Johnson, interview with Stacey Petrey, audio recording, Lexington, VA, March 29, 2017.

3. Jeffrey Sonnenfeld, "CEO Exit Schedules: A Season to Stay, a Season to Go," *Fortune*, May 6, 2015, http://fortune.com/2015/05/06/ceo-tenure-cisco/.

4. Kristen Frasch, "CEO Turnover vs. CEO Tenure: Two Takes," HRE Daily page, January 25, 2016, http://blog.hreonline.com/2016/01/25/ceo-turnover-vs-ceo-tenure-two-takes/.

5. Whitney Johnson, "Marshall Goldsmith and Whitney Johnson—CEOs Should Have Term Limits," YouTube, February 22, 2017, https://www.youtube.com/watch?v=RBBh1z4U3uE.

Conclusion

1. Paul Nunes and Tim Breene, *Jumping the S-Curve: How to Beat the Growth Cycle, Get on Top, and Stay There* (Boston: Harvard Business Review Press, 2011), 152–156.

2. Ann Lamott, *Help, Thanks, Wow: The Three Essential Prayers* (New York: Penguin, 2012), 86.

3. Benjamin Franklin, *The Autobiography of Benjamin Franklin*.

4. "Maker Culture," *Wikipedia*, last modified October 16, 2017, https://en.wikipedia.org/wiki/Maker_culture.

INDEX

ACKNOWLEDGMENTS

*Most people return small favors, acknowledge medium
ones, and repay greater ones—with ingratitude.*

—**Benjamin Franklin**

It's not possible to express the depth of my gratitude for the help I've received, but I will try.

To Clayton Christensen—the intellectual giant on whose shoulders I stand—I am so grateful for the decade I spent working with and learning from you.

Thank you to Sarah Green Carmichael, my sponsor and editor extraordinaire at Harvard Business Review Press. This book wouldn't have happened without you. Thank you also to Tim Sullivan and the rest of the team. It's been a pleasure and a privilege to work with you.

I owe a huge debt of gratitude to editor Heather Hunt for her help throughout the writing process, from proposal to finishing touches. You are a brilliant writer. I'm glad we reconnected after our days at the Orem Public Library.

Thank you to the dynamic duo Amy Jameson and Brandon Jameson: Amy for her keen editorial eye and Brandon for his unerring design sensibility. You've been wonderful partners for more than fifteen years.

Thank you to Amy Humble for helping this cobbler "make her own shoes" when it comes to building and scaling a business. To Macy Robison, there's no descriptor because you do so many things: from building our website to developing courses to helping to manage the daily beast that is this growing business. And to Sally Harker. I am so grateful for your pinch-hitting during the early part of this book.

A huge shout-out to Marla Gottschalk, who took the reins in building the S-Curve Locator and Disruptive Strengths Indicator, and to Christine Goodwin, whose massive analytical and design prowess has hustled them into something wonderful. (I'm also grateful for your spot-on insights after reading an early draft of this book.)

Thank you to Amy Gray, who has taught me so much about speaking. And to David Klatt for his mentorship on podcasting. Many of the interviews we did together found their way into this book. And thank you to old and new friends Alex Osterwalder, Patrick Hodgdon, Franz Busse, Melissa Davis, and Jake Smith. Your review of early drafts of this book improved it tremendously.

I am deeply indebted to Marshall Goldsmith for his sponsorship and for the Marshall Goldsmith 100 program. Because of you, my life has been changed for good.

To my mother, because she wanted to write a book—she made me think I could.

To my husband, Roger, our children, David and Miranda, my many dear friends (you know who you are), and to God. From the deepest place in my heart, thank you.

ABOUT THE AUTHOR

WHITNEY JOHNSON's research and work in disruptive innovation shapes how individuals and corporations manage change. After publishing her book *Disrupt Yourself: Putting the Power of Disruptive Innovation to Work* (2015), Johnson was recognized as one of the world's fifty most influential management thinkers by Thinkers50 in 2015 and again in 2017. Through speaking, writing, coaching, and consulting, she synthesizes the key levers of change and shares how to use them effectively.

In addition to *Build an A-Team* and *Disrupt Yourself*, she is the author of *Dare, Dream, Do* (2012). She speaks about innovation initiatives and has delivered keynote speeches to audiences across the globe about disruption, innovation, teamwork, and organizational change. Johnson is also a frequent contributor to *Harvard Business Review*, a LinkedIn Influencer, and host of the *Disrupt Yourself* podcast. She is a member of the original cohort of Marshall Goldsmith's 100 Coaches.

She is cofounder with Clayton Christensen of the Disruptive Innovation Fund, where they invested in and led the $8 million seed round for Korea's Coupang, currently valued at more than $5 billion. Johnson was involved in fund formation, capital raising, and the development of the fund's strategy. During her tenure, the CAGR of the fund was 11.98 percent versus 1.22 percent for the S&P 500.

Previously, Johnson was an *Institutional Investor*–ranked equity research analyst for eight consecutive years and was rated by Starmine as a superior stock picker. As an equity analyst, Johnson's stocks under coverage included América Móvil (NYSE: AMX), Televisa (NYSE: TV), and Telmex (NYSE: TMX), which accounted for roughly 40 percent of Mexico's stock market capitalization exchange.

Johnson is shaping how organizations embrace and manage disruption by leading individuals and teams up the S curve of change. She focuses on harnessing the core competencies required to build a team that can leverage opportunities and unite when faced with adversity.

To learn more about Johnson's work, you can sign up for her newsletter, tune into her podcast, or contact her about speaking, consulting, and coaching at whitneyjohnson.com.

48 - Ask if Amazon will send execs
   to CPM.